# Teach Yourself

# VISUALLY™

## PowerPoint® 2003

Visual®

Nancy Muir

WILEY

Wiley Publishing, Inc.

# Teach Yourself VISUALLY™
# PowerPoint® 2003

Published by
**Wiley Publishing, Inc.**
111 River Street
Hoboken, NJ 07030-5774

Published simultaneously in Canada

*Library of Congress Control Number: 2005936633*

ISBN-13: 978-0-7645-9983-5

ISBN-10: 0-7645-9983-6

Manufactured in the United States of America

10 9 8 7 6 5 4 3 2 1

## Trademark Acknowledgments

## Contact Us

For general information on our other products and services please contact our Customer Care Department within the U.S. at 800-762-2974, outside the U.S. at 317-572-3993 or fax 317-572-4002.

For technical support please visit www.wiley.com/techsupport.

**WILEY**

Wiley Publishing, Inc.

**Sales**

Contact Wiley
at (800) 762-2974 or
fax (317) 572-4002.

# Praise for Visual Books

"Like a lot of other people, I understand things best when I see them visually. Your books really make learning easy and life more fun."

John T. Frey (Cadillac, MI)

"I have quite a few of your Visual books and have been very pleased with all of them. I love the way the lessons are presented!"

Mary Jane Newman (Yorba Linda, CA)

"I just purchased my third Visual book (my first two are dog-eared now!), and, once again, your product has surpassed my expectations.

Tracey Moore (Memphis, TN)

"I am an avid fan of your Visual books. If I need to learn anything, I just buy one of your books and learn the topic in no time. Wonders! I have even trained my friends to give me Visual books as gifts."

Illona Bergstrom (Aventura, FL)

"Thank you for making it so clear. I appreciate it. I will buy many more Visual books."

J.P. Sangdong (North York, Ontario, Canada)

"I have several books from the Visual series and have always found them to be valuable resources."

Stephen P. Miller (Ballston Spa, NY)

"Thank you for the wonderful books you produce. It wasn't until I was an adult that I discovered how I learn – visually. Nothing compares to Visual books. I love the simple layout. I can just grab a book and use it at my computer, lesson by lesson. And I understand the material! You really know the way I think and learn. Thanks so much!"

Stacey Han (Avondale, AZ)

"I absolutely admire your company's work. Your books are terrific. The format is perfect, especially for visual learners like me. Keep them coming!"

Frederick A. Taylor, Jr. (New Port Richey, FL)

"I have several of your Visual books and they are the best I have ever used."

Stanley Clark (Crawfordville, FL)

"I bought my first Teach Yourself VISUALLY book last month. Wow. Now I want to learn everything in this easy format!"

Tom Vial (New York, NY)

"Thank you, thank you, thank you...for making it so easy for me to break into this high-tech world. I now own four of your books. I recommend them to anyone who is a beginner like myself."

Gay O'Donnell (Calgary, Alberta, Canada)

"I write to extend my thanks and appreciation for your books. They are clear, easy to follow, and straight to the point. Keep up the good work! I bought several of your books and they are just right! No regrets! I will always buy your books because they are the best."

Seward Kollie (Dakar, Senegal)

"Compliments to the chef!! Your books are extraordinary! Or, simply put, extra-ordinary, meaning way above the rest! THANK YOU THANK YOU THANK YOU! I buy them for friends, family, and colleagues."

Christine J. Manfrin (Castle Rock, CO)

"What fantastic teaching books you have produced! Congratulations to you and your staff. You deserve the Nobel Prize in Education in the Software category. Thanks for helping me understand computers."

Bruno Tonon (Melbourne, Australia)

"Over time, I have bought a number of your 'Read Less - Learn More' books. For me, they are THE way to learn anything easily. I learn easiest using your method of teaching."

José A. Mazón (Cuba, NY)

"I am an avid purchaser and reader of the Visual series, and they are the greatest computer books I've seen. The Visual books are perfect for people like myself who enjoy the computer, but want to know how to use it more efficiently. Your books have definitely given me a greater understanding of my computer, and have taught me to use it more effectively. Thank you very much for the hard work, effort, and dedication that you put into this series."

Alex Diaz (Las Vegas, NV)

# Credits

**Project Editor**
Maureen Spears

**Acquisitions Editor**
Jody Lefevere

**Product Development Manager**
Lindsay Sandman

**Copy Editor**
Tricia Liebtig

**Technical Editor**
Diane Koers

**Editorial Manager**
Robyn Siesky

**Manufacturing**
Allan Conley
Linda Cook
Paul Gilchrist
Jennifer Guynn

**Illustrators**
Steve Amory
Matthew Bell
Elizabeth Cardenas-Nelson
Kristen Corley
Ronda David-Burroughs
Cheryl Grubbs
Jake Mansfield
Rita Marley
Paul Schmitt

**Book Design**
Kathie Rickard

**Production Coordinator**
Maridee Ennis

**Layout**
Beth Brooks
Jennifer Heleine
Amanda Spagnuolo

**Screen Artist**
Jill A. Proll

**Proofreader**
Arielle Mennelle

**Quality Control**
Amanda Briggs

**Indexer**
Richard T. Evans

**Vice President and Executive Group Publisher**
Richard Swadley

**Vice President and Publisher**
Barry Pruett

**Composition Director**
Debbie Stailey

## About the Author

**Nancy Muir** is a full time writer of business and technology books. She has authored over 50 books, including *The Young Person's Guide to Character Education*, *Online Distance Learning For Dummies*, and *The 10 Minute Guide to Motivating People*. On the desktop application side, Nancy has written dozens of books on products such as Excel, Word, and PowerPoint, as well as books on the Internet and wireless technology.

Nancy lives with her wonderful husband Earl in a beautiful home they have built together in the Pacific Northwest. Their dog, Bryn, takes them for long walks on a regular basis, and their cat, Wellington, is in charge of the entire family.

## Author's Acknowledgments

Special thanks go out to publisher, Barry Pruett, and to acquisitions editor, Jody Lefevere, for allowing me to take on this project; to project editor, Maureen Spears, for her dedication and patience in guiding this project from start to finish; to copy editor, Tricia Liebtig, for ensuring that there were no grammatical errors; to technical editor, Diane Koers, for checking all things technical; and finally to the graphics and production teams at Wiley for their hard work and dedication in making this book a success.

## Dedication

To Earl, my partner and friend who supports me in all I do, loves me with all his heart, and keeps our lives happy day in and day out.

# Table of Contents

## chapter 4 Work with Outlines

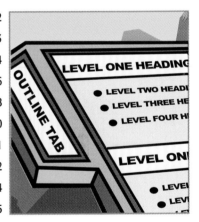

## chapter 5 Work with Slide Layouts

# Table of Contents

## chapter 6  Using Design Templates and Color Schemes

## chapter 7  Using Masters

# chapter **8** Add Graphics and Drawings

# Table of Contents

# chapter 11 Set Up and Run a Slide Show

# chapter 12 Print Presentations

# chapter 13 Give Presentations Online

# Table of Contents

 **chapter 14   Finalize and Make a Presentation**

**chapter 15   Customize PowerPoint**

## PowerPoint Keyboard Shortcuts

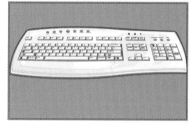

## Online Resources

# How to use this book

Do you look at the pictures in a book or newspaper before anything else on a page? Would you rather see an image instead of read about how to do something? Search no further. This book is for you. Opening Teach Yourself VISUALLY PowerPoint 2003 allows you to read less and learn more about the Excel programs.

## Who Needs This Book

This book is for a reader who has never used this particular technology or software application. It is also for more computer literate individuals who want to expand their knowledge of the different features that PowerPoint has to offer.

## Book Organization

Teach Yourself VISUALLY PowerPoint 2003 has 15 chapters and two appendices.

Chapter 1 covers PowerPoint basics, including navigating through the various views and working with the task panes and toolbars.

Chapter 2 shows you how to work with a PowerPoint presentation.

In Chapter 3, you learn how to make your presentation look sharp by formatting it with styles, color and bulleted lists.

In Chapter 4, you work with outlines including moving headings up or down in your presentation, collapsing and expanding outlines, and sending an outline to Word.

Chapter 5 explains how to work with slide layouts and shows you how to add elements such as pictures, charts, and tables.

Chapter 6 covers design templates and color schemes that give your presentation a professional touch.

In Chapter 7, you learn how to use masters to make global changes to your slides.

Chapter 8 shows you how to work with graphics and drawings, including how to insert AutoShapes, text boxes, WordArt, and more.

In Chapter 9, you organize slides by rearranging, deleting, and duplicating them.

Chapter 10 introduces animation features. You learn how to apply and play animation schemes and insert action buttons.

In Chapter 11 you set up and run your slide show.

Chapter 12 explains the ins and outs of printing your presentation, outline, speaker's notes, and handouts.

Chapter 13 shows you how set up and publish Web presentations.

In Chapter 14, you learn how to finalize and make a presentation, including how to navigate through your slides and annotate them with the pointer.

You learn how to customize your presentation in Chapter 15, which discusses many advanced PowerPoint settings, creating new toolbars, and recording macros.

The Appendices provide valuable keyboard shortcuts and resources to make your work with PowerPoint efficient and successful.

## Chapter Organization

This book consists of sections, all listed in the book's table of contents. A section is a set of steps that show you how to complete a specific computer task.

Each section, usually contained on two facing pages, has an introduction to the task at hand, a set of full-color screen shots and steps that walk you through the task, and a set of tips. This format allows you to quickly look at a topic of interest and learn it instantly.

Chapters group together three or more sections with a common theme. A chapter may also contain pages that give you the background information needed to understand the sections in a chapter.

## What You Need to Use This Book

To perform the steps in this book, you need the following:

- A personal computer with a 233-MHz or faster processor
- 128 MG of RAM or more
- 400 MB of hard disk space to install PowerPoint 2003
- A CD-ROM or DVD drive
- A Super VGA monitor (800x600 resolution or higher and 256 colors)
- Microsoft Windows XP or Windows 2000 with Service Pack 3
- An Internet connection

## Using the Mouse

This book uses the following conventions to describe the actions you perform when using the mouse:

### Click

Press your left mouse button once. You generally click your mouse on something to select it on the screen.

### Double-click

Press your left mouse button twice. Double-clicking something on the computer screen generally opens whatever item you have double-clicked.

### Right-click

Press your right mouse button. When you right-click anything on the computer screen, the program displays a shortcut menu containing commands specific to the selected item.

### Click and Drag, and Release the Mouse

Move your mouse pointer and hover it over an item on the screen. Press and hold down the left mouse button. Now, move the mouse to where you want to place the item and then release the button. You use this method to move an item from one area of the computer screen to another.

## The Conventions in This Book

A number of typographic and layout styles have been used throughout Teach Yourself VISUALLY PowerPoint 2003 to distinguish different types of information.

### Bold

Bold type represents the names of commands and options that you interact with. Bold type also indicates text and numbers that you must type into a dialog box or window.

### Italics

Italic words introduce a new term and are followed by a definition.

## Numbered Steps

You must perform the instructions in numbered steps in order to successfully complete a section and achieve the final results.

## Bulleted Steps

These steps point out various optional features. You do not have to perform these steps; they simply give additional information about a feature.

## Indented Text

Indented text tells you what the program does in response to you following a numbered step. For example, if you click a certain menu command, a dialog box may appear, or a window may open. Indented text may also tell you what the final result is when you follow a set of numbered steps.

### Notes

Notes give additional information. They may describe special conditions that may occur during an operation. They may warn you of a situation that you want to avoid, for example the loss of data. A note may also cross reference a related area of the book. A cross reference may guide you to another chapter, or another section with the current chapter.

## Icons and Buttons

Icons and buttons are graphical representations within the text. They show you exactly what you need to click to perform a step.

 You can easily identify the tips in any section by looking for the TIPS icon. Tips offer additional information, including tips, hints, and tricks. You can use the TIPS information to go beyond what you have learned in the steps.

## Operating System Difference

The figures and steps in this book depict the Windows XP operating system. If you are using Windows 2000, your own screens may look differently. PowerPoint 2003 does not work on earlier versions of the Windows operating system.

# 1

# PowerPoint Basics

Get ready to discover the basics of starting and moving around a PowerPoint presentation. In this chapter, you learn about the various elements of the PowerPoint screen, and how to get help when you need it.

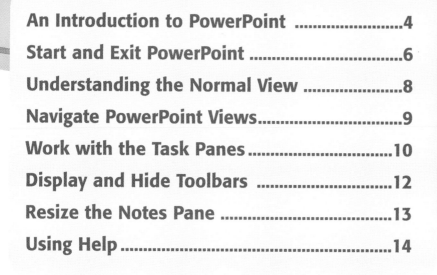

# An Introduction to PowerPoint

PowerPoint is a program that provides various views and tools you can use to build a presentation that includes both words and graphics. Here is what you can do with PowerPoint.

## Build an Outline

You can type the text part of your presentation in the Outline tab. Each slide is represented by a topic in the outline. Many slides contain a topic title and subheads for that topic in the form of bullet points. These bullets summarize the main points you want to make about each topic.

## Add Content

You can add content to your presentation either in the Outline view or on individual slides in the Slide pane. You can also insert text boxes that allow you to add text to slides that do not appear in the presentation outline.

## Choose a Slide Design and Layout

*Slide designs* apply preset design elements such as colors, background graphics, and text styles to your slides. *Slide layouts* are predesigned sets of information that you want to include on a slide; for example, a title and text layout inserts placeholders just for text, whereas a title and content layout includes a title and graphic placeholder that might contain an illustration or table.

## Work with Masters

Masters allow you to add content that you want to appear on every (or almost every) slide in one place. This saves you from having to add repetitive content, such as your company logo, to each and every slide manually. Masters are often used to place graphics or footers in a presentation, for example.

## Format Text

When you have entered text for your presentation, you can format that text in various ways. You can change the font, increase the font size, and add effects such as bold and italic to the text. Note that you can modify each individual set of selected text, or apply text styles globally using masters.

## Organize Slides

When you have created several slides, you should reorganize them to get the correct sequence for your presentation. You can do this in the Slide Sorter view. Thumbnails of slides are displayed which you can move, duplicate, hide, or delete from your presentation.

## Set Up Your Show

In addition to text and graphics, PowerPoint allows you to add narrations, animations, and transitions to your slides. You can record a *narration* that plays when you give your presentation. *Animations* give the appearance of movement to an element; for example, a graphic may appear to fade onto the screen gradually. A *transition* is an effect that controls how a new slide is displayed; for example, it can slide in from the corner of the slide.

## Run a Show

After you enter the contents, set up the slide design, and add special effects, you are ready to run your show. You can navigate through a show in Slide Show view. A set of tools helps you control your presentation, and even make notes on your slides as you present them.

# Start and Exit PowerPoint

You can start PowerPoint from the Windows Start menu. When you open PowerPoint, you see a blank presentation. It is ready for you to enter your presentation contents.

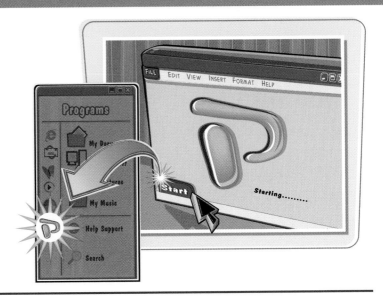

## Start and Exit PowerPoint

### START POWERPOINT

① From the Windows desktop, click **Start**.

② Click **All Programs**.

③ Click **Microsoft Office**.

④ Click **Microsoft Office PowerPoint 2003**.

*Note: If you purchased PowerPoint as a standalone product, simply click All Programs, and then click PowerPoint 2003.*

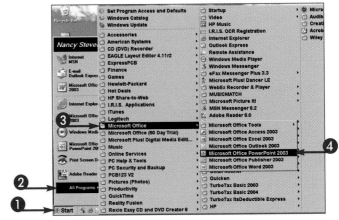

A PowerPoint presentation appears with a blank slide.

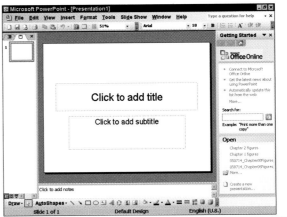

## EXIT POWERPOINT

**1** Click **File**.

**2** Click **Exit**.

*Note:* Only the most frequently used commands on this menu appear initially; if necessary, wait a moment for the entire menu to appear.

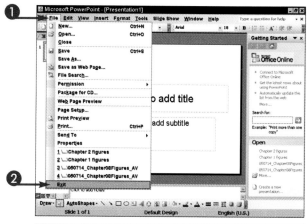

The program closes and you return to the Windows desktop.

### TIP

**Is there a quicker way to open PowerPoint?**

You can place a shortcut to PowerPoint on your Windows desktop. Double-click the PowerPoint icon to open the program. To create a shortcut:

**1** Click **Start**.

**2** Click **All Programs**.

**3** Right-click **Microsoft Office PowerPoint 2003**.

**4** Click **Create Shortcut**.

A second Microsoft Office PowerPoint 2003 appears in the submenu.

**5** Click and drag the shortcut to the Windows desktop.

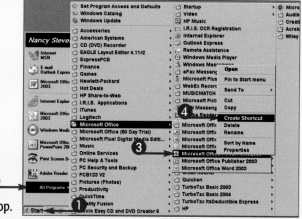

# Understanding The Normal View

PowerPoint offers several views you can display to work on different aspects of your presentation. You will probably work in Normal view most often to design the layout of objects on each slide; enter your presentation contents in an Outline tab; or enter speaker's notes for each slide.

**Slides Pane**

You can use this area of Normal view to manipulate the various elements of the slide such as graphic objects, text, and animations.

**Notes Pane**

Under the Slide pane is the Notes pane where you can enter speaker notes associated with the displayed slide.

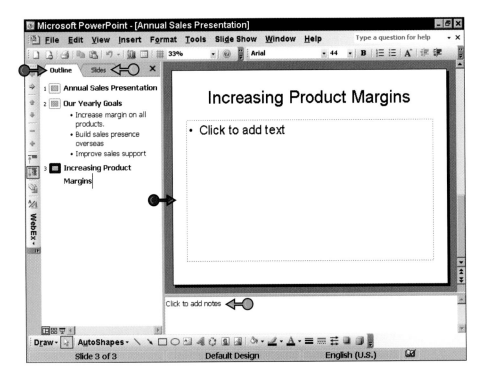

**Outline Tab**

You can use this tab to enter text for your presentation in a familiar outline format. Top-level headings in an outline become slide titles, and subheadings become bullet lists. For a quick overview of all your slides, you can also click the Slides tab, which is next to the Outline tab.

**Slide Tab**

For a quick overview of all your slides, you can also click the Slides tab, which is next to the Outline tab.

In addition to Normal view, you can use the Slide Sorter view to organize slides in a presentation and Slide Show view to run your presentation.

**Moving among the PowerPoint views allows you to get different perspectives on your presentation. You can use the View menu, or three always-available view icons to switch views quickly.**

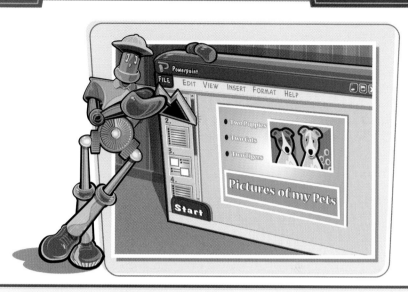

### Navigation Buttons

Change views by clicking one of these icons. From left to right they take you to **Normal view** (⬚), **Slide Sorter** view (⬚), and **Slide Show** view (⬚). You can also choose commands from the View menu to switch views.

### Slide Show View

Slide Show view is where you run your slideshow. Slides appear full screen with a panel of tools you can use to navigate the show, draw annotations on the slides, or display your speaker notes. To display this view, you can click the **Slide Show** icon (⬚). To exit this view, you can press Esc.

### Slide Sorter View

You can click the **Slide Sorter View** icon (⬚) to display this view. You can use this view to reorganize your slides or quickly delete or duplicate slides. If you double-click a slide in this view, you are taken to Normal view with that slide displayed in the Slide pane.

### Task Pane

This pane contains tools for performing commonly used PowerPoint tasks. You can click the **Other Task Panes** icon (⬚) to display a menu of other available panes. See the section "Work with the Task Pane" for more information.

The task pane is an area you can display on the right side of the PowerPoint screen. There are more than a dozen task panes available, each containing different sets of tools you can use to get things done in PowerPoint.

### Work with the Task Pane

1 If the Task pane is not displayed, click **View**.

**Note:** If the Task pane is already displayed, skip to step **3**.

2 Click **Task Pane**.

You can also press Ctrl + F1 to display the task pane.

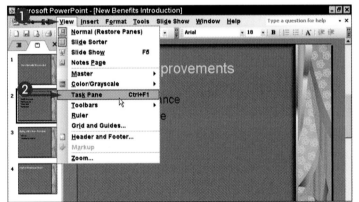

The task pane appears.

3 Click the **Other Task Panes** icon (▼).

**Note:** This button is labeled with the name of whatever task pane is currently displayed; by default, the Getting Started task pane appears when you first display the pane.

4 Click the task pane you want to display.

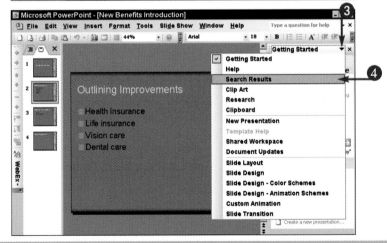

The new task pane appears.

⑤ Click the **Back** () or **Forward** ( ) icon to move to the previous or next task pane.

⑥ Click **Close** ( ).

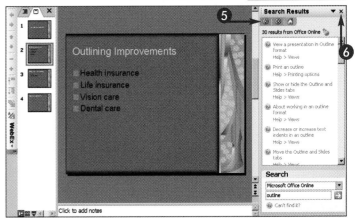

The task pane is removed from Normal view.

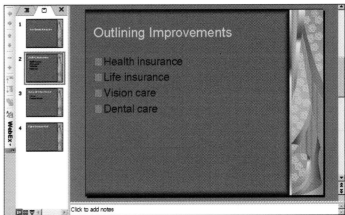

**TIPS**

**What does the Document Updates command in the Other Task Panes menu display?**

You can view updates to shared documents in this task pane only if you have made a document available in a shared workspace. See Chapter 14 for more about shared workspaces.

**Why do some items in task panes appear in blue?**

Those items are links you can click to display additional information in the task pane; go to an online location; or to display a dialog box to perform a certain task.

There are 13 toolbars you can display in PowerPoint. You do not need to use them at all times, so you may want to hide certain toolbars when you are not using them.

**You may want to hide toolbars if they take up too much of the screen. They make it harder for you to work with slide content because you can see less of your slides.**

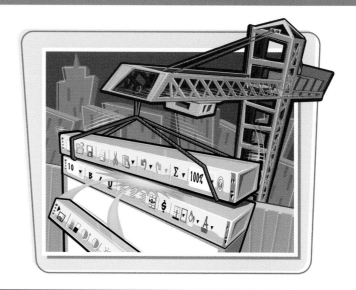

## Display and Hide Toolbars

❶ Click **View**.

❷ Click **Toolbars**.

❸ Click the name of any hidden toolbar.

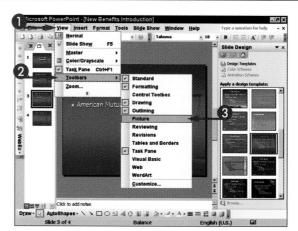

● The toolbar is displayed.

❹ Right-click in the toolbar area.

❺ Click a currently displayed toolbar.

The toolbar disappears from the screen.

The Notes pane is where you enter speaker notes. This area appears just under a slide in Normal view. You can resize the Notes pane to make it easier to enter information into it.

**You can print just the notes pages from your presentation. See Chapter 12 for more about how to print.**

## Resize the Notes Pane

**①** Click and drag down.

*Note: If you click and drag up, the pane enlarges.*

The pane disappears.

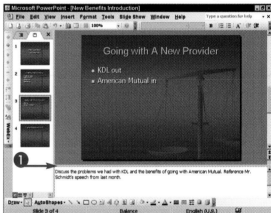

**②** Click **View**.

**③** Click **Normal (Restore Panes)**.

The Notes pane reappears.

With PowerPoint Help you can search for help topics, go to Microsoft Online, or contact Microsoft to get answers to your questions. There is also a useful table of contents where you can search for information by category.

## Using Help

① Click **Help**.

② Click **Microsoft Office PowerPoint Help**.

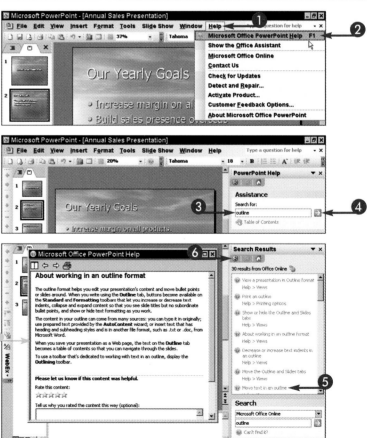

The Help task pane appears.

③ Type a word or phrase.

④ Click the **Start Search** icon (▣).

The search results appear.

⑤ Click any blue text.

● The topic is displayed in a separate window.

⑥ Click the **Back** icon (▣).

The Help home page appears.

**7** Click **Table of Contents**.

The Table of Contents appears.

**8** Click a main topic.

**9** Click a subtopic to see a list of help information.

*Note: Main topics have a small folder ( ) next to them; subtopics have an open book ( ) next to them; and detailed topic information is indicated by a question mark symbol ( ) next to the item.*

**10** Click a detailed topic.

The detailed topic is displayed.

**11** Click the **Close** icon (⊠) to close the detailed topic window.

**12** Click the **Back** icon (◉).

The Help home page appears.

● You can click this link to go to Microsoft Office Online help.

● You can click this link to get information and advice about PowerPoint.

● You can click this link to update help options in the task pane from the Web.

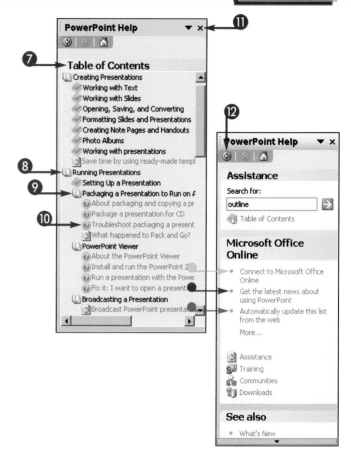

**TIPS**

**How can I contact Microsoft for help?**
Display the **Help** task pane and click the **Contact Us** link. You may need to scroll down in the main Help page to see this link. This displays a Web page with information about various ways to get in touch with Microsoft.

**Is there a shortcut for displaying the Help task pane?**
Yes. Simply press F1 and the task pane is displayed. Pressing F1 is also a way to return to the Help main page from other areas of Help.

# CHAPTER 2

# Presentation Fundamentals

Before you build a presentation, you should know how to create a presentation file. After you create and save a file, you need to work with those files, which you learn about in this chapter.

# Start a New Presentation

After you open PowerPoint, there are a few options for creating a new presentation. For example, you can start a blank presentation, or use an existing design template.

**There is also a feature called AutoContent Wizard that provides suggested content based on the type of presentation you are building.**

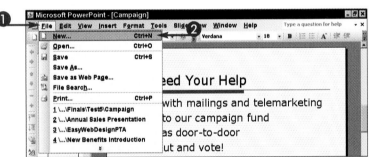

**OPEN A BLANK PRESENTATION**

① Click **File**.

② Click **New**.

The New Presentation task pane appears.

③ Click the **Blank Presentation** link.

A blank presentation opens and the Slide Layout task pane appears.

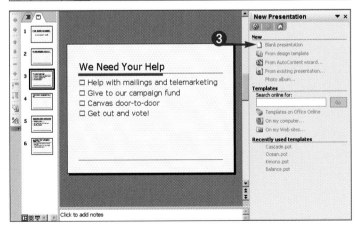

**OPEN A TEMPLATE**

**1** Click **File**.

**2** Click **New**.

**3** In the New Presentation Task pane, click **From Design Template**.

● A blank presentation opens and the Slide Design task pane appears.

**4** Click a design thumbnail.

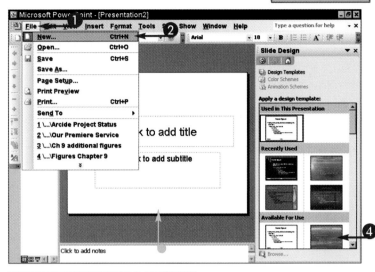

The design is applied to the presentation.

**TIPS**

**How does AutoContent Wizard work?**
When you click the **From AutoContent Wizard** link in the New Presentation task pane, a wizard screen appears. It walks you through the process of specifying the type of presentation you are creating, for example, an in-person training or a Web marketing presentation. Based on that input, PowerPoint creates a presentation with placeholder text on a series of pre-created slides. You can then use that content to guide you through creating a presentation that fits your particular needs. This gives you a great head start on building presentation content.

**Is there a quicker way to start a certain type of presentation besides walking through the AutoContent Wizard?**
Yes. Click the **On my computer** link in the New Presentation task pane and on the Presentations tab of the New Presentations dialog box that appears, click a related file. Click **OK** to create the presentation.

# Save a Presentation

After you create a presentation and have put some work into it, you should save it. Saving a PowerPoint file is much like saving any other Windows program file: you need to specify the location to save the file to, and give it a name.

**With a presentation, you also have the option to package it to save it to a CD. This includes a copy of the PowerPoint viewer with the file for easy playback. Learn more about this in Chapter 14.**

Save a Presentation

**①** Click **File**.

**②** Click **Save**.

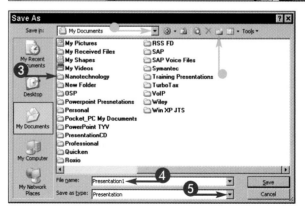

The Save As dialog box appears.

**③** Click the folder where you want to save your file.

● You can click the Create New Folder icon (🗀) to create a new folder or click the Save in 🔽 to display a list of folders.

**④** Type a file name.

**⑤** Click here to select a file format.

*Note: If you want to save to the default PowerPoint 2003 format, you do not have to perform steps 5 and 6.*

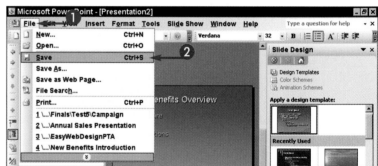

**6** Click a format.

**7** Click **Save**.

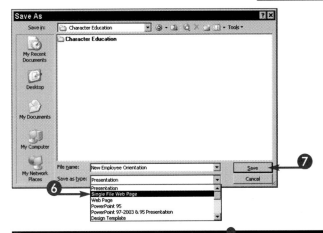

The dialog box closes and you return to the presentation.

● The new file name is now listed in the title bar.

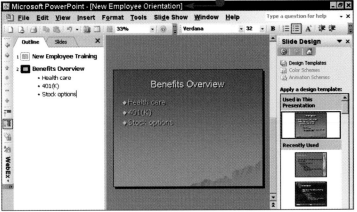

TIPS

**I save presentations in a specific folder all the time. Is there a quicker way to locate that folder in the Save As dialog box?**

Yes. You can click the **My Recent Documents** button in the Save As dialog box to locate your folder. You can also click the **Tools** menu in the Save in toolbar, and then click **Add to My Places** to add the currently selected folder to the Save in bar. You can then click the folder's icon in the Save in bar to locate the folder quickly.

**Is there a shortcut to save to a folder I just saved another presentation to?**

Yes. Click the **My Recent Documents** icon in the Save in bar. The folder you most recently saved a presentation to appears.

# Open an Existing Presentation

After you have saved and closed a presentation, you must locate it and reopen it the next time you want to use it.

**If you used a presentation recently, the quickest way to open it is in the list of recently used files at the bottom of the File menu.**

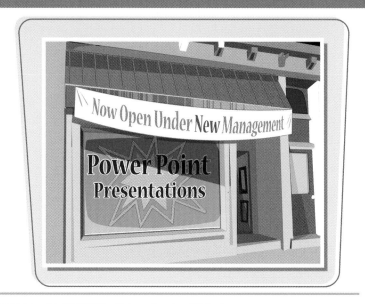

## Open an Existing Presentation

① Click **File**.

② Click **Open**.

● If you used the file recently, you can also click it in the list at the bottom of the File menu.

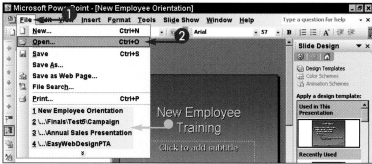

The Open dialog box displays.

③ Click to display the correct folder.

④ Click the file name.

⑤ Click **Open**.

● Alternatively, you can type the presentation name here; as you type, PowerPoint highlights the matching file.

PowerPoint opens the file.

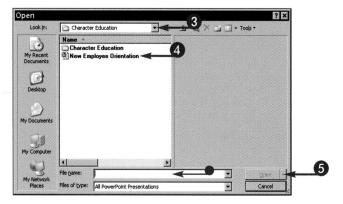

When you finish working with a presentation and have saved the file, you can close it but still keep PowerPoint open to work with other presentations.

**If you have not already saved the file, PowerPoint prompts you to save it before you can close the presentation. For more on saving a presentation, see the section " Save a Presentation."**

## Close a Presentation

① Click **File**.

② Click **Close**.

● Alternatively, you can click the **Close** icon (⊠).

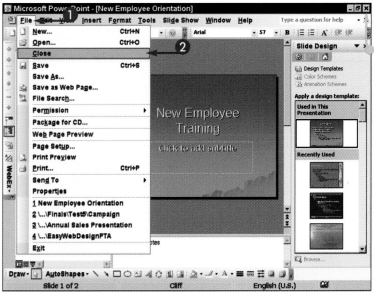

A message may appear asking if you want to save changes.

③ Click **Yes**.

● If you do not want to save the changes to your presentation, you can click **No**.

The file closes, but PowerPoint remains open.

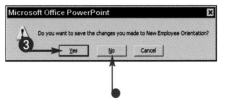

# Delete a Presentation

There may come a time when you have no more need for a presentation. Perhaps it is out of date, or you decide that you do not need to keep a back-up copy any longer. By deleting a file, you free up some disk space in your computer.

**If there is any chance that you may need the presentation again, consider placing a copy of it on a CD or other media before deleting it from your computer.**

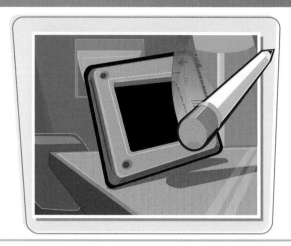

## Delete a Presentation

① From the Windows desktop, click **Start**.

② Click **My Documents**.

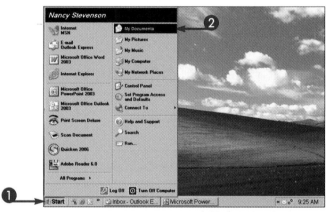

The Windows Explorer window appears, showing the contents of the My Documents folder.

③ Double-click the folder containing the file.

④ Click the file.

⑤ Click **File**.

⑥ Click **Delete**.

The Confirm File Delete dialog box appears.

⑦ Click **Yes**.

PowerPoint deletes the file.

● You can click ⊠ to close the My Documents window.

# Arrange Presentation Windows

You can easily display several presentations at once, for example if you want to compare their contents. You can do this by using commands in the Window menu.

**It is not recommended that you display more than three windows at once. More than three, and you cannot see enough of each presentation to make this feature useful.**

## Arrange Presentation Windows

① Open two or more presentations.

② Click **Window**.

③ Click **Arrange All**.

The windows display side by side.

④ Click **Window**.

⑤ Click **Cascade**.

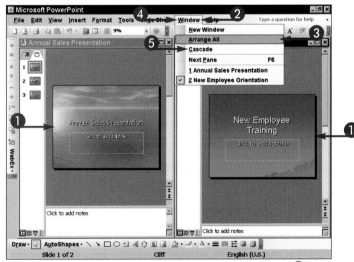

The windows are displayed overlapping each other, just like a deck of cards.

You can click and drag the window title bars to arrange them.

⑥ Click either window's **Close** icon (✕).

The selected window closes.

⑦ Click the remaining window's **Maximize** icon (◻).

It appears full screen again.

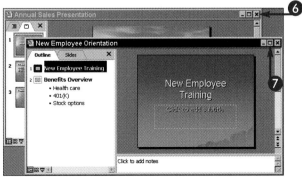

# Find a Presentation

Sometimes you want to open a file but you forget what you named it or what folder you saved it to. You can use a search feature to locate the file.

You can also use the search feature on the Windows Start menu to locate a file in a similar fashion.

① Open the Open dialog box.

*Note:* For more information, see the section "Open an Existing Presentation."

② Click **Tools**.

③ Click **Search**.

The File Search dialog box appears.

④ Type in the search text box.

*Note:* This is text that appears somewhere in the file title or document contents.

⑤ Click here and select the location to search.

*Note:* My Computer is selected by default.

⑥ Click here and select the type of file to search for.

*Note:* All Office file types and Web files are selected by default.

⑦ Click **Go**.

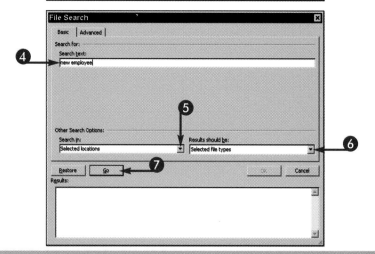

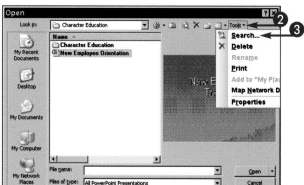

PowerPoint searches the selected location and displays the results in the File Search window.

**8** Click a file name.

**9** Click **OK**.

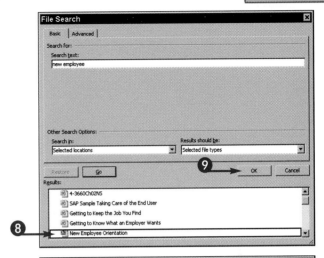

You return to the Open dialog box.

● The selected file name appears here.

**10** Click **Open**.

The file opens.

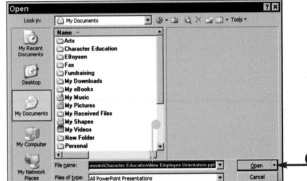

 **TIPS**

**I remember how many slides the presentation contained and the last date I saved it, but nothing else. Any tips on how to find it?**

Click the **Advanced** tab of the File Search dialog box. Here you can specify a wide variety of properties for the file, such as the number of slides in the presentation and the date last saved, or the date last printed.

**Is there a way to check the detailed properties of a file returned by a search without opening it?**

Yes. Right-click the file name in the search results and click **Properties**. The Properties dialog box appears. In the Properties dialog box, you can view all the information you need to know about your file.

# 3

# Type and Format Presentation Text

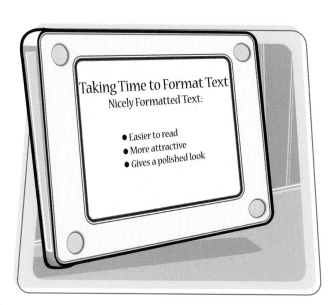

Words form the basis of any presentation; taking the time to format text can pay off in many ways. Nicely formatted text is easier to read and helps make your slides more attractive and polished.

You use PowerPoint to build a presentation slide by slide. Those slides, shown in order, make up your presentation. Different slide types serve different functions in your presentation.

## Title Slide

The *title slide* is the first slide. There is usually just one title slide in a presentation. Typically the title slide includes the presentation title or topic, and a subtitle. The subtitle might be the presenter's name or the presenting company's name, or it might be the date and location of the presentation.

## Title and Text Slide

A *title and text slide* is perhaps the most frequently used slide layout. The layout controls what placeholders appear on a slide. For more about layouts see Chapter 5. This is also referred to as a bullet-list slide because it contains a title and a bulleted list. The bulleted list consists of the key points the speaker wants to make about a specific topic. Bullet points should be concise and clear to help guide the viewer through the presentation.

## Content Slide

You can add various kinds of content to your presentation using a content layout. For example, you can add tables, charts, clip art, pictures, diagrams, or media clips (sound or video). Content is often used as a design element. You might insert a corporate logo or picture or video to add visual pizzazz or emphasize a point. You can also use tables, charts, and diagrams to present data in a visual way.

## Summary Slide

You can generate a summary slide that lists the titles of all the slides in your presentation. For more on generating a summary slide, see Chapter 4. This is often the second slide in a presentation, following the title slide. A summary slide is an overview of what is covered to help the viewer grasp the flow of the presentation. Some people like to add a duplicate summary slide at the end of a presentation as a review of what has been covered.

You use various text formatting tools in PowerPoint to apply effects to selected text. The Formatting toolbar provides most of the tools you need; or, you can make formatting changes in the Font dialog box.

## Change the Font

When you type text on a slide, it is formatted with a font that is determined by whatever slide design is applied. See Chapter 6 for more about slide designs. You can change the font for selected text or for all text in a title or bulleted list. The font is the style of the text and gives a certain look and feel to your presentation content such as formal or informal.

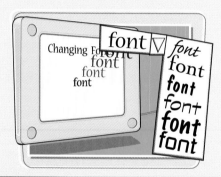

## Change Text Color

You can use text color for both a design and a practical purpose. In designing your slides, text color should be attractive to the eye. However, the most important thing about text color is that it be readable against whatever background you have selected for your slides. Yellow text on a white background is unreadable, for example. You can also use color on selected text to add emphasis.

## Resize Text

The size of text in a presentation is important because it can make it more or less readable. You can modify the size of text to match the environment where you make the presentation. Viewed at a kiosk or in a small conference room, the text can be smaller and still be read. Viewed in a huge ballroom where the person at the back may be many yards away, larger text is helpful.

## Add Effects

There are some styles you can apply to text, such as bold, italic, shadow, emboss, and underline. These add emphasis and should be used sparingly. However they can call the viewer's attention to important words or phrases throughout your presentation.

# Add a Slide

When you open a new presentation, PowerPoint creates a blank title slide. To build your presentation, you can add as many slides as you like.

**The number of slides in your presentation is determined by the number of topics you want to cover and is limited by the time you have available to cover them.**

## Add a Slide

1 With a presentation open (either blank or existing), click **Insert**.

2 Click **New Slide**.

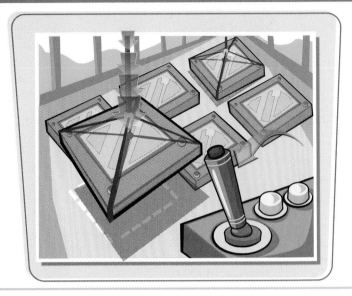

● A new blank slide with the title and text layout appears.

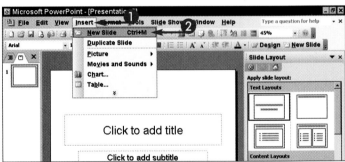

As you build your presentation you may decide you do not need a particular slide. In this case you can simply delete that slide.

**It is common to build one presentation and then use it as the basis for other presentations. In this case you may need to delete several slides that are irrelevant or out of date.**

## Delete a Slide

① With a PowerPoint presentation open in Normal view, click the slide you want to delete in the Slides or Outline tab.

*Note: For more on Normal view, see Chapter 1.*

This example shows the selection in the Outline tab.

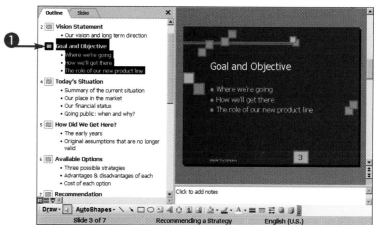

② Click **Edit**.

③ Click **Delete Slide**.

The slide is deleted from the presentation.

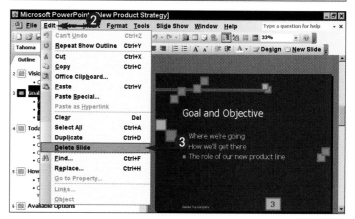

# Navigate Slides

After you create several slides in your presentation, you can move among them in several ways. You can use the buttons on various scrollbars to display the slide, and then select any displayed slide in the Slides or Outline tab, or in Slide Show view.

## LOCATE A SLIDE USING THE SCROLLBAR

1. With a PowerPoint presentation open in Normal view, click and drag the scrollbar to scroll through slides.

2. Click the **Next Slide** icon (⬇) to go to the next slide.

3. Click the **Previous Slide** icon (⬆) to go to the previous slide.

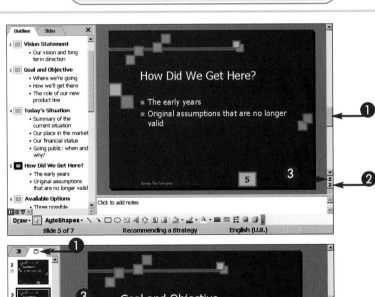

## NAVIGATE USING THE SLIDES TAB

1. Click here to display the Slides tab.

2. Click and drag the scrollbar to scroll through the slides.

3. Click a slide.

   The slide is selected in the Slides tab and displayed in the Slide pane.

## NAVIGATE USING THE OUTLINE PANE

**1** Click the **Outline** tab.

**2** Click and drag the scrollbar to scroll through the slides.

**3** Click a slide.

The slide is selected in the Outline tab and displayed in the Slide pane.

## NAVIGATE IN SLIDE SORTER VIEW

**1** Click the **Slide Sorter View** icon (🔠).

The Slide Sorter view is displayed.

**2** Click and drag the scrollbar to scroll through the slides.

**3** Click a slide.

The slide is selected.

*Note: To display the selected slide in Normal view, double-click it.*

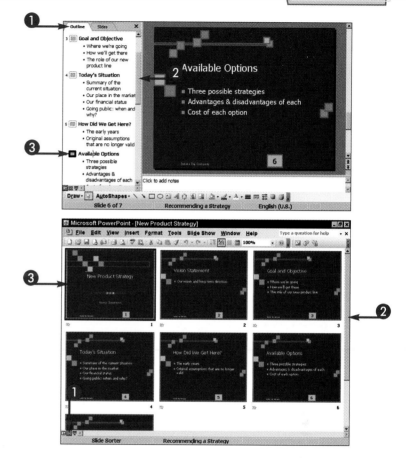

**There are no scrollbars in the Slides or Outline tabs. Why?**

If PowerPoint can display all the slides in your presentation without scrolling down or up, it does not display scrollbar.

**Is there a way to see more slides in Slide Sorter view so it is easier to find the one I want to navigate to?**

Yes. You can click **View**, and then **Zoom**. Select a lower zoom percentage to display more slides at a time. For example, if you have displayed slides at 100 percent of their size, click 50 percent or 33 percent to shrink the slides and fit more on your screen.

# Type and Edit Text on a Slide

You can type text on a slide using placeholders. There are three types of text placeholders: title, text, and subtitle. You select the placeholder and then start typing. You can also go back and edit text you have already typed.

## Type and Edit Text on a Slide

### ENTER TITLE OR SUBTITLE TEXT

**1** With a PowerPoint presentation open in Normal view, click any title or subtitle placeholder.

*Note: For more on Normal view, see Chapter 1.*

The placeholder opens for editing.

**2** Type your text.

**3** Click outside the placeholder.

The text is saved.

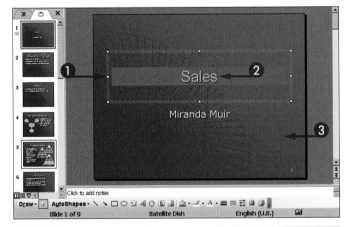

### ENTER BULLET TEXT

**1** Click a text placeholder.

The placeholder opens for editing.

**2** Type a bullet point.

**3** Press `Enter`.

Your cursor moves to the next bullet point in the list.

**4** Type the second bullet point.

You can continue steps **3** and **4** until you have entered all bullet points for the slide.

**5** Click outside the placeholder.

The text is saved.

## EDIT TEXT

**1** Click a title, subtitle, or text placeholder.

**2** Click anywhere within existing text.

A thin, vertical line appears where you clicked.

**3** Press `Backspace` to delete text to the left of the cursor.

**4** Type any text you want to add.

The text is entered at the cursor's position.

**5** Click and drag over the text.

Text is selected and highlighted.

**6** Press `Delete`.

The selected text is deleted.

### TIPS

**Why does my placeholder say "Click to add text"? Will this appear if I print or run my presentation?**

That is simply an instruction to let you know that this placeholder currently has no entered text. The words and the placeholder neither print nor appear when you present the slide show.

**When I type text in the Outline tab, where does it appear?**

Text that you type in the Outline appears on the currently displayed slide. The upper heading in an outline corresponds to the title placeholder on the slide. Lower-level headings become the bullet items in the text placeholder.

# Format Text Color and Style

Color adds flair to any presentation. You can use color to make your text more readable and more attractive. You can select colors from a standard palette or work with custom colors. You can use text styles such as bold or shadow to add emphasis.

Format Text Color and Style

**CHANGE TEXT COLOR**

① Click a placeholder to select it.

② Click and drag to select text to be formatted.

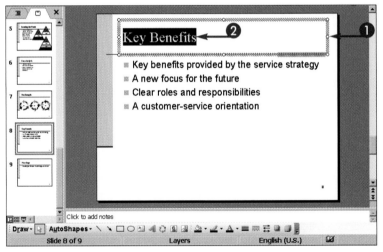

③ Click **Format**.

④ Click **Font**.

The Font dialog box appears.

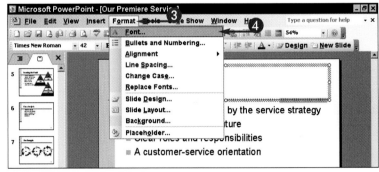

**5** Click here.

A color palette appears.

● To select another standard color or a custom color, you can click **More Colors** below the palette.

**6** Click a color.

The palette disappears.

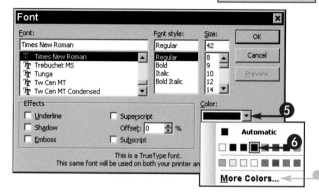

**CHANGE TEXT STYLE**

**1** In the Font Style area, click to select Regular, Bold, Italic, or Bold Italic.

In this example, Italic is selected.

● You can select an Effects option (☐ changes to ☑) to select other text effects.

**2** Click **OK**.

The text color or effects are applied.

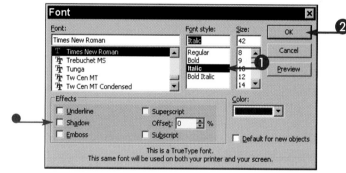

**What is the difference between applying formats with the Formatting toolbar or the Font dialog box?**

The Font dialog box lets you apply several formats at one time from a central location. You can use the tools on the Formatting toolbar to apply one attribute at a time. If you only want to change one thing, for example, color or size of text, the fastest way is to select the text and click the appropriate tool on the toolbar.

**What are superscript and subscript?**

These formats either raise (superscript) or lower (subscript) the selected text a set distance from the regular text. Superscript and subscript are often used for footnote or scientific notation—such as $4^2$ representing 4 to the second power.

# Format Text Font and Size

Applying a font gives text a certain style. Some fonts are playful, others more formal. Fonts are divided into two types: serif, such as Times New Roman; and sans serif, such as Arial. The right text size is important for readability.

Format Text Font and Size

**CHANGE TEXT FONT**

① Click a placeholder.

   The placeholder opens for editing.

② Click and drag to select text to be formatted.

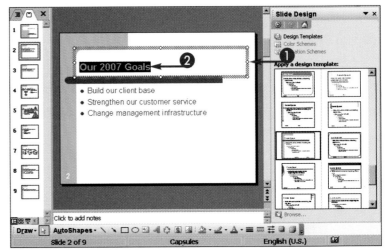

③ Click **Format**.

④ Click **Font**.

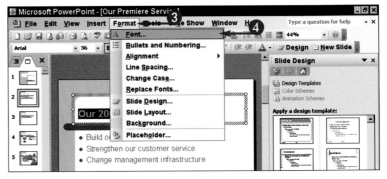

The Font dialog box appears.

**5** Click a font.

**6** Type a font size.

*Note: You can also click and drag the scrollbar thumb to locate a font size and click it.*

**7** Click **OK**.

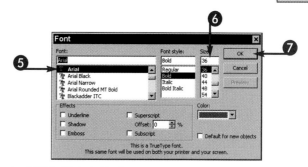

● The new formatting is applied to the text.

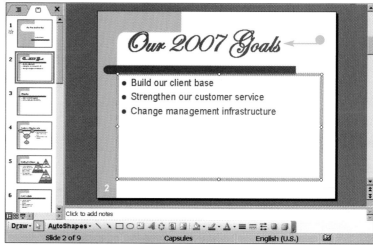

### What does the TT symbol to the left of fonts in the font list mean?

TT stands for TrueType. This is a WYSIWYG — What You See Is What You Get — font technology. This means that the outline you see for the font on-screen accurately reflects the appearance of your printed font.

### Are there limitations to how large or small type can be?

You can type whatever font size you like, with the lower limit being 1 and no known upper limit. As a rule of thumb, 72 points is approximately 1 inch tall. But remember, the whole point of type size is to keep the type readable for the viewer. A very small text size will do nobody any good; a huge text size may make text merely a design element.

# Cut, Copy, and Paste Text

Sometimes as you are editing your presentation you will want to move text from one slide to another. You can do this using the Cut, Copy, and Paste functions. Cut removes text from one place; Copy makes a copy of it; Paste places either cut or copied text into another location.

## CUT TEXT

**①** Click a placeholder containing text.

The placeholder opens for editing.

**②** Click and drag to select text.

**③** Click **Edit**.

**④** Click **Cut**.

The selected text is removed and placed on the Windows Clipboard.

## COPY TEXT

**①** Click a placeholder containing text.

The placeholder opens for editing.

**②** Click and drag to select text.

**③** Click **Edit**.

**④** Click **Copy**.

The selected text is copied to the Windows clipboard.

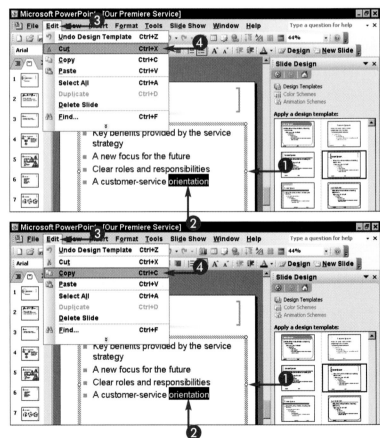

42

**PASTE TEXT**

**1** Locate the slide or placeholder where you want to paste the text.

***Note:*** *See the section "Navigate Slides" to locate the destination slide.*

**2** Click a placeholder.

The placeholder opens for editing.

**3** Click where you want to paste the text.

A vertical line appears.

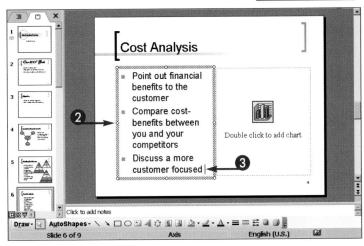

**4** Click **Edit**.

**5** Click **Paste**.

The cut or copied text is pasted into the placeholder.

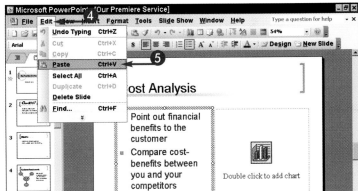

**TIPS**

**There is a phrase I want to copy and paste into several slides. Is there a shortcut to do that?**

Yes. You can press
Ctrl + C to copy and
Ctrl + X to cut text from a slide. Anything you cut or copy is placed on the Windows clipboard. Until you cut or copy something else, it remains on the clipboard and you can paste it as many times as you like.

**I cut some text and then changed my mind. Is there anything I can do to get it back?**

If you just cut the text, you can click **Edit**, and then **Undo Cut** to undo the action. Or, you can just click **Edit**, and then **Paste** and paste it back in place. If you saved the file or performed several actions since cutting the text, it is likely that it is lost and you will have to retype it.

# Format Bullet Lists

Bullet lists are the heart of any presentation. They contain key points the presenter wants to make. You can format bullet lists to use different styles of bullets. For example, you might format bullets in a presentation for a gardening business as a flower or tree, or use a check mark for the bullets in a list of action steps for a project.

## Format Bullet Lists

### APPLY A STANDARD BULLET STYLE

1 Click a text placeholder.

The placeholder opens for editing.

2 Click and drag to select the bulleted text you want to format or click the placeholder border to select all bulleted text.

3 Click **Format**.

4 Click **Bullets and Numbering**.

The Bullets and Numbering dialog box appears.

5 Click a bullet style.

6 Click **OK**.

The bullet style is applied to the selected bulleted text.

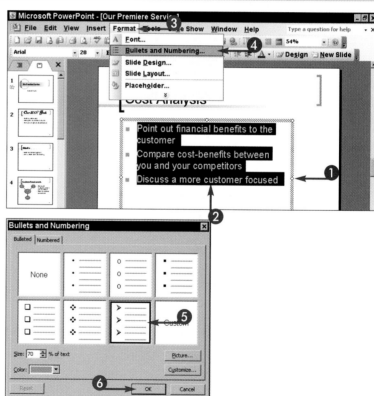

## APPLY A CUSTOM BULLET STYLE

**1** With the Bullets and Numbering dialog box open, click **Customize**.

**Note:** *To open the Bullets and Numbering dialog box, see steps 1 to 4 on the previous page.*

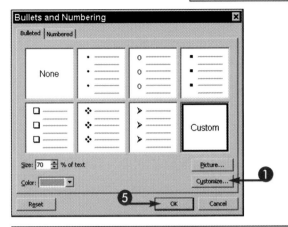

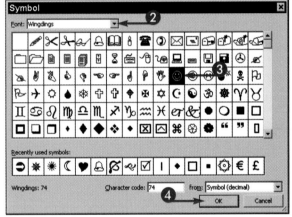

The Symbol dialog box appears.

**2** Click here and select a font.

**3** Click a symbol.

**4** Click **OK**.

The Symbol dialog box disappears.

**5** Click **OK** in the Bullets and Numbering dialog box.

The dialog box closes and the new bullet style is applied.

**TIPS**

### How can I make the bullets larger?

In the Bullets and Numbering dialog box, there is a setting for size. This setting is expressed in percentage of text, meaning the bullet size is set relative to the size of the text. If you increase the text size, for example, the bullet size increases proportionally. Click the spinner arrows (⬍) on this setting to the size you want, and then click **OK** to apply the sizing.

### Can I apply a new bullet style to every bullet in the presentation without having to change it on each and every slide?

Yes. You can use the Master Slide feature to make formatting changes that apply to every slide in the presentation. Master slides are covered in detail in Chapter 7.

# Using the Spell Check Feature

When you type text in a presentation, you should check that text for spelling accuracy. Not all of us are spelling bee winners! Luckily PowerPoint offers a Spell Check feature to make this simple. You can use it to check the spelling of all words throughout the presentation.

**①** Click **Tools**.

**②** Click **Spelling**.

The Spelling dialog box appears with the first questionable word listed.

**③** Perform one of the available actions.

● You can click a suggested alternate spelling.

● You can type the correct spelling here and click **Change**.

● You can click to leave the spelling as is.

● You can click to leave all instances of this spelling as they are.

● The spelling check proceeds to the next questionable word.

④ Repeat step **3** until the spell check is complete.

A dialog box appears notifying you that the spell check is complete.

⑤ Click **OK**.

The dialog box closes and the spell check is complete.

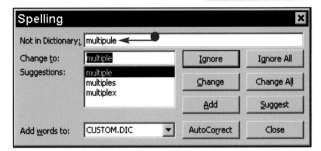

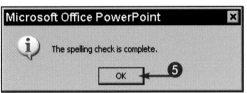

## Is it possible to spell check just one specific word?

Yes. Select the word before running the spell check. The spell check starts with the word you selected. When you take the appropriate action and continue, the spell check goes to the next questionable word. Click the **Close** icon (☒) to close the Spelling dialog box at that point. An even faster method is just to right-click any word with a squiggly red underline, which is PowerPoint's way of suggesting there is a misspelling, and select the suggested correction from the list that appears.

## Is there a way to prevent PowerPoint from flagging a particular word as a misspelling? Our company name is an acronym and it flags it every time!

In the Spelling dialog box, click **Add**. This adds the word to PowerPoint's dictionary, so it recognizes it as a legitimate spelling in all presentations going forward.

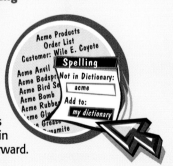

# Using the Research Feature

As you type text in a presentation, you may need to check words or facts. With an Internet connection you can use the Research feature to search reference books and research sites for relevant information.

Using the Research Feature

1 Click **Tools**.

2 Click **Research**.

The Research Task pane appears.

3 Type a term to research.

4 Click and select a source to search.

5 Click the **Start Searching** icon (⬛).

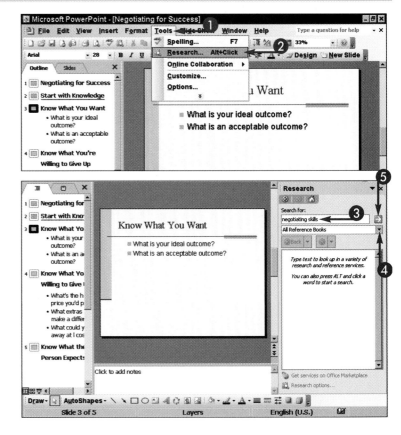

- Search results appear.

**6** Click a link.

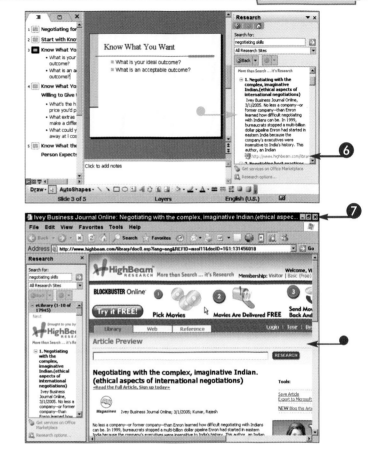

- Additional information or a Web site appears, depending on the type of link.

**7** Click ⊠.

The Research Task pane or your browser closes.

**Can I specify which research sites PowerPoint will check?**

Yes. With the Research task pane displayed, click the **Research Options** link. A dialog box appears with a list of all resources. Only some are selected by default. Select any items you want to add to searches (☐ changes to ☑).

**I followed a link but what was there was of no interest. Is there a way to go back to the original item that was displayed?**

Yes. Click the **Back** icon (⊙) or click the arrow to the right of ⊙ to display a list of all the items you have looked at in this search. Click the one you want to see again to go to it.

# CHAPTER

# Work with Outlines

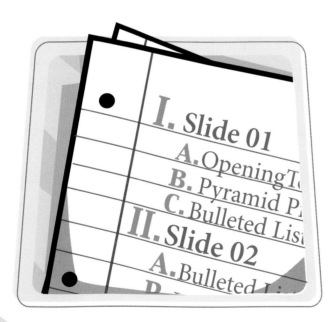

The Outline tab is the easiest place to enter most of the text in your presentation. It uses a simple outline hierarchy of headings you are probably used to already.

# Hide and Display the Outline Tab and Toolbar

The Outline tab helps you work with an outline when focusing on presentation contents. However, because many of the things you can do in the Outline tab can also be done with click and drag or keyboard functions, you may want to close the Outline tab now and then to see more of the currently selected slide when you are focusing on slide design.

You can then restore Normal view to display the Outline tab again. You can also choose to hide or display the Outlining toolbar, which offers tools for working with various levels of outline text for similar reasons. The Outline task tab appears in Normal view.

Hide and Display the Outline Tab and Toolbar

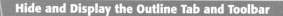

**HIDE AND DISPLAY THE OUTLINE TASK TAB**

① Click the **Close** icon (⊠) on the Outline tab, if it is displayed.

The Outline tab is hidden.

② Click **View**.

③ Click **Normal (Restore Panes)**.

The Outline tab reappears.

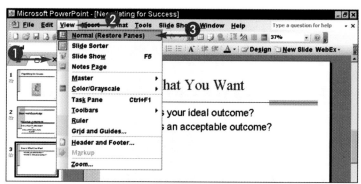

**DISPLAY THE OUTLINING TOOLBAR**

① Click **View**.

② Click **Toolbars**.

③ Click **Outlining**.

The Outlining toolbar appears.

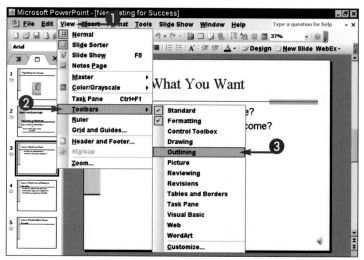

You can enter presentation text in the Outline tab, or directly on a slide in the Slide pane in Normal view. When you do, it is important that you understand how the contents of the outline and each slide relate.

## One Heading, One Slide

Every upper level heading, that is a heading at level 1 in the outline, is the title of a slide. When you type text in a title placeholder it appears as a level 1 heading in the outline. When you type a level 1 heading in the outline, it appears in the title placeholder.

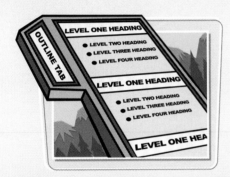

## Where Graphics Live

Graphics never appear in the outline. You place graphics on slides in the Slide pane. Likewise text boxes that you draw on a slide and their contents are not reflected in the outline.

## Bullet to Bullet

The second level of headings in an outline becomes the bullets in the text placeholder on the corresponding slide. If you have more than one level of bullets in the outline, there will be multiple levels of bullets on the slide, and vice versa.

## A Slide to Summarize It All

A Summary slide is built automatically from the titles of every slide in the presentation. You do not have to enter a thing to generate a Summary slide.

# Enter Presentation Content in an Outline

When you enter text in the Outline tab, it is something like using the Outline view of a word processing program. You enter text, and then use tools on the Outlining toolbar to demote headings — this means to move them to a lower level in the outline hierarchy — or to promote them to a higher level.

**The first slide in an outline is automatically formatted as the Title slide; new slides that you add have the Title and Text format applied automatically, though you can change this.**

## Enter Presentation Content in an Outline

**①** Click **File**.

**②** Click **New**.

The New Presentation task pane appears.

**③** Click the **Blank Presentation** link.

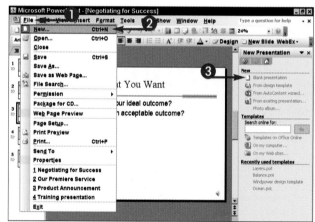

A new, blank presentation opens.

**④** Click the **Outline** tab.

**⑤** Click in the outline.

**⑥** Type a heading.

**⑦** Press Enter.

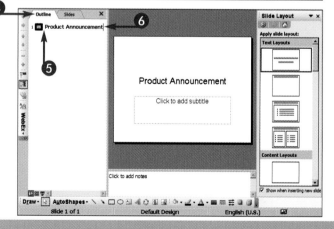

The heading appears as the title of the first slide and a second blank slide is created.

⑧ Type a second heading.

The heading appears at the upper level of the outline by default.

⑨ Press Enter .

⑩ Type a third heading.

⑪ Press Tab .

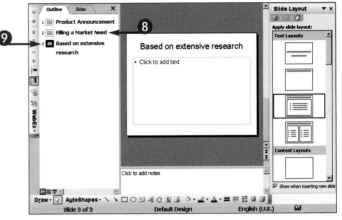

• The heading moves down one level to become part of the text placeholder on the second slide.

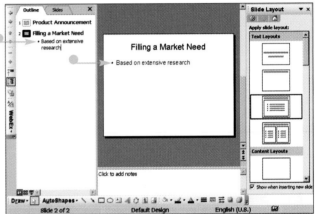

**With a lot of text I have trouble reading my outline. Is there a way to enlarge the Outline tab?**

Yes. Simply move your mouse to the right edge of the pane and click and drag the edge to the right. Notice that the Slide pane shrinks in size to accommodate the change. To reduce the size of the pane again, just click and drag to the left. If you drag too far the pane disappears, but you can click the **View** menu to restore to Normal view.

**Can I print just the presentation outline?**

Yes. It is often useful to just see the text part of the outline. See Chapter 12 for information about how to do this. You can also send the outline to Word and print it from there; this is covered later in this chapter. However, remember that no graphics or text box contents will print if you only print the outline.

# Move Slides Around an Outline

Presentations are like any other kind of writing in that they evolve in drafts. It is not always possible to know the exact order for slides when you are first creating them. That is when you have to rearrange the slides in your outline. You can do this by using the Outlining toolbar, or by using the click and drag method.

**For more on the Outline tab and Outlining toolbar, see the section "Hide and Display the Outline Tab and Toolbar."**

## Move Slides Around an Outline

① Click the **Slide** icon (🖼) for the slide you want to move.

② Click the **Move Up** (🔼) or **Move Down** (🔽).

The entire slide moves up or down in the outline.

③ Click the bullet of a second level heading to select it.

④ Click 🔼 or 🔽.

The heading moves up or down and can even move from one slide to another.

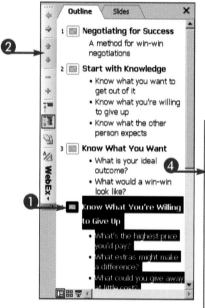

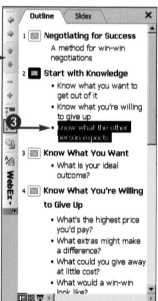

⑤ Click and drag a bullet to move it in the outline.

● A line appears showing where the heading will be placed.

⑥ Release the mouse button.

● The heading appears in its new position.

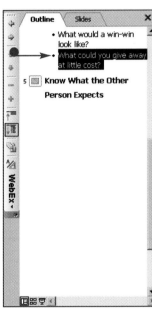

 **TIPS**

**My Move Up tool seems to be missing. Is there a way to make changes to the Outlining toolbar?**

Yes. If you have a tool you seldom use and do not want to display it, you can click the arrow at the bottom of the toolbar to display the Toolbar Options menu. Click **Add or Remove Buttons**, and then click **Outlining**. The current tools are displayed. Click any tool you want to include, and then click outside the menu. The tool appears on the toolbar again.

**Is there a way to move headings up or down in an outline using the keyboard?**

Yes. Click the heading and press [Alt] + [Shift] + [↑] to move it up in the outline. Press [Alt] + [Shift] + [↓] to move the heading down in the outline.

# Promote and Demote Items

An important part of building your outline involves moving upper level headings so that they become subheadings (called *demoting*) and moving lower level headings up to become higher level topics (called *promoting*). You can do this using the Promote and Demote tools on the Outlining toolbar, or by clicking and dragging headings.

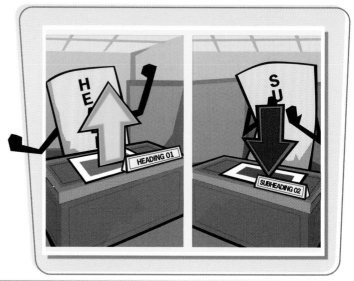

**1** Click anywhere in a heading.

**2** Click the **Demote** icon (⬇).

● The heading moves down one level in the outline hierarchy.

**3** Click anywhere in a heading other than a level 1 heading.

**4** Click the **Promote** icon (⬆).

You can click ⬆ and ⬇ more than once to move the heading more than one level in the outline.

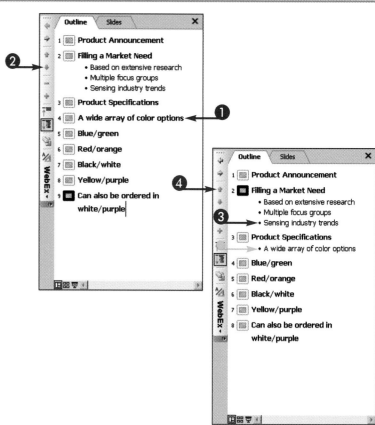

● The heading moves up one level in the outline hierarchy.

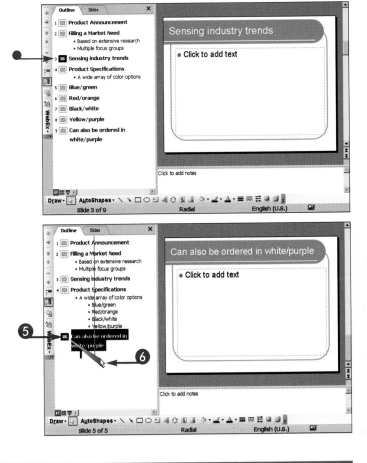

⑤ Click 🖳, or the bullet next to a heading.

⑥ Drag the heading to the right.

The heading moves down as many levels as you drag it.

 **TIPS**

**Is there a keyboard shortcut for promoting or demoting headings in a PowerPoint outline?**

Yes. Click in a heading and press Tab to demote a heading; or press Shift + Tab to promote a heading in the outline.

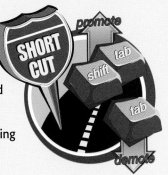

**Can you promote and demote headings from the Slide pane?**

Yes, however you cannot promote or demote a title. Click in a heading in the text placeholder on the slide and click either 🔼 and 🔽 on the Outlining toolbar or press Tab or Shift + Tab on the keyboard. The change in outline level occurs both on the slide and in the outline.

# Collapse and Expand an Outline

Especially with larger presentations, it is sometimes helpful to collapse an outline to reveal only higher level headings or to expand it to look at the detail in just one section. Collapsing subheadings helps you to scroll through the presentation more quickly.

**You can also collapse or expand a specific set of slides by selecting them before using these procedures.**

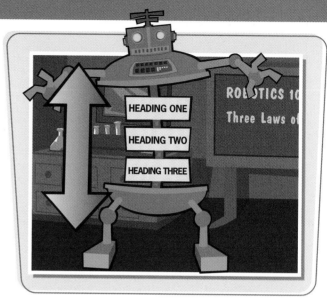

## Collapse and Expand an Outline

① Click a heading with subheads beneath it.

② Click the **Collapse** icon (⬜).

The subheadings are hidden.

③ Click the **Expand** icon (⬜).

The subheadings reappear.

④ Click the **Collapse All** icon (⬜).

All subheadings in the entire outline are hidden.

⑤ Click the **Expand All** icon (⬜).

All subheadings in the entire outline are displayed.

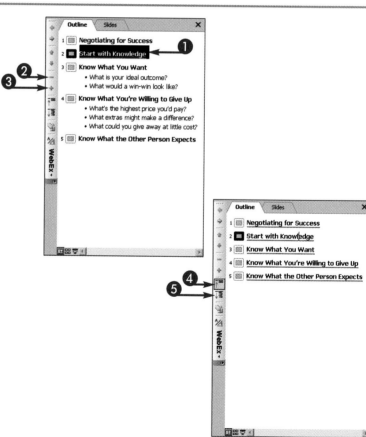

After you enter text for a presentation, you must edit that text to polish it or make corrections if you have typos or other errors. Editing an outline is much like editing text anyplace else in PowerPoint.

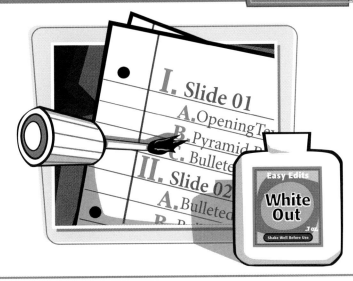

## Edit Outline Content

1. Click within a heading at the point where you want to add or delete text.

2. Add or delete the text.

   Pressing Delete deletes the letter to the right of your cursor.

   Pressing Backspace deletes the text to the left of your cursor.

3. Click anywhere in a heading and type new or replacement text.

4. Click the slide or bullet icon to select a heading.

5. Press Delete.

   ● All heading text is deleted.

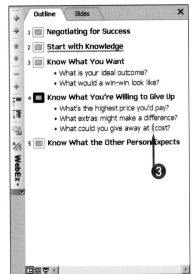

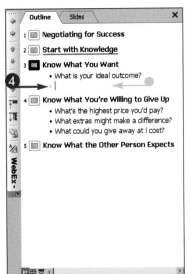

# Add a
# Summary Slide

It is often useful at the beginning or end of a presentation to give the viewers an overview of all the topics you are about to cover or which you have just covered. This repetition helps keep viewers oriented as you work through your topics.

**A quick way to list all the upper level headings in your presentation is to create a Summary slide. You can then copy and paste it to also appear at the end of your presentation, if you like.**

## Add a Summary Slide

❶ Click **Edit**.

❷ Click **Select All**.

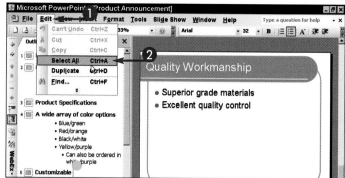

● All slides in the presentation are selected.

❸ Click the **Summary Slide** icon (🖼).

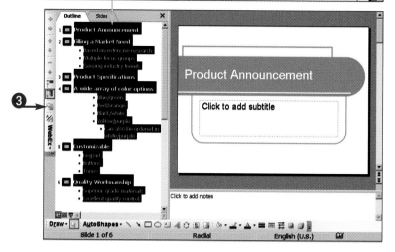

● A Summary slide is generated at the beginning of the outline.

④ Click the **Copy** icon ().

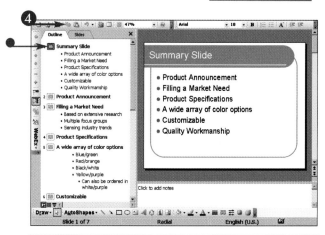

⑤ Click at the end of the last heading in the outline.

⑥ Click the **Paste** icon ().

● A copy of the Summary slide appears at the end of the presentation.

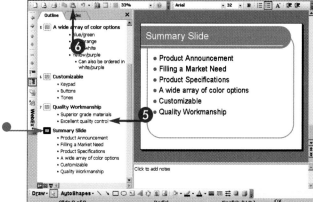

---

 **TIPS**

**Is there a way to create a Summary slide for one subsection of slides in my presentation?**

Yes. Just select those slides before clicking the **Summary Slide** icon (). Whatever slides are selected are included in the resulting slide, which appears before the first slide in the sequence of slides you selected.

**Can a Summary slide be demoted just like any other slide?**

Yes. Just use any of the methods described in this chapter: clicking the **Demote** icon () on the Outlining toolbar, pressing Tab, or clicking and dragging the heading to the right.

# Send an Outline to Word

When you have typed some or all your text into PowerPoint, you may want to work with it in a more familiar tool, such as Microsoft Word. Here you can make your edits using Word's tools, or print out or repurpose the contents for other documents.

**You can also create your original outline in Word and send it from Word to PowerPoint in a similar fashion.**

① Click **File**.

② Click **Send To**.

③ Click **Microsoft Office Word**.

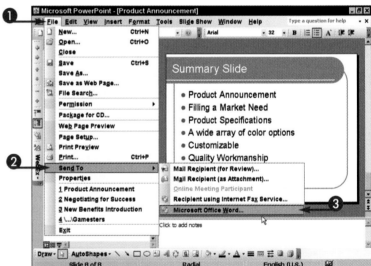

The Send To Microsoft Office Word dialog box appears.

④ Click the **Outline Only** option (📄 changes to 📄).

⑤ Click **OK**.

Word opens displaying a document containing the PowerPoint outline.

As you refine your presentation now and then you may decide not to use some material. In that case you might have to delete a slide. You can easily do that from the Outline tab.

**You can also delete slides using the Slide tab, or in Slide Sorter view. For more on the Slide tab, see Chapter 3. For more on the Slide Sorter view, see Chapter 9.**

## Delete a Slide in an Outline

① Click anywhere within the contents of a slide in the **Outline** tab.

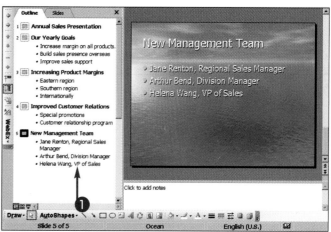

② Click **Edit**.

③ Click **Delete Slide**.

The entire slide is deleted.

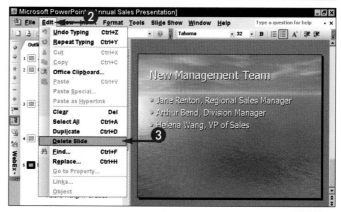

# CHAPTER
# 5

# Work with
# Slide Layouts

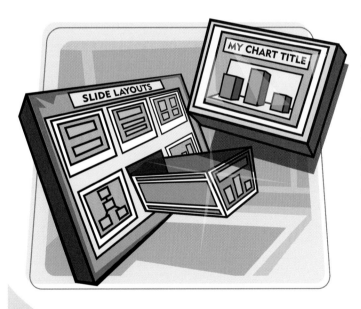

Slides are made up of various types of placeholders. The slide layout consists of the combination and arrangement of these placeholders. You can edit the contents of the placeholders to create your presentation, which may be a combination of text and various types of visual content.

# Understanding Layouts and Placeholders

Most presentations are made up of a combination of slide titles, slide text in the form of bulleted lists, and graphic elements. These standard elements are preset for you in selectable slide layouts.

### Types of Slide Layouts

Slide layouts are arranged in the Slide Task pane in various groupings. For example, Text Layouts include any layout with a combination of titles, subtitles, or bulleted lists. Content Layouts contain placeholders that you can use to insert any one of six types of graphic elements such as a chart or picture. Text and Content Layouts provide combinations of text and graphic placeholders in various arrangements. One final category is called Other Layouts, and it contains some text elements plus a content placeholder that you can use to insert one type of graphic, such as a table or diagram.

### Placeholders

The various slide layouts are prearranged sets of placeholders. Placeholders contain either text or content in the form of graphic elements, but not both. You can click a text placeholder and type or edit text. You can click a content placeholder and use the icons in it to insert or edit a visual element. You can also move placeholders around the slide to design a more attractive arrangement.

### The Slide Layout Task Pane

You can use the Slide Layout Task pane to apply slide layouts. Whenever you insert a new slide, this task pane automatically appears. You can apply a layout to the currently selected slide in Normal or Slide Sorter view. By default, when you open a new presentation, a single slide is created with the Title Slide Layout, containing a title and subtitle for the presentation. Thereafter, every time you insert a new slide, it uses the Title and Text Layout with a title and bulleted list placeholder.

### Slide Layouts Are Flexible

Often after you apply a layout, you find that you want to resize and move placeholders around the slide. You can easily do that by clicking and dragging the handles around the edges of the placeholder in or out to resize it, or clicking the outer edge and dragging the placeholder to another location. Placeholders can be deleted from a layout, but this is not really necessary: If a placeholder has no content in it, it is not visible when you print or show your presentation.

By default, the Slide Layout task pane appears whenever you insert a new slide. However, you may want to display it at other times to change a layout from the default.

**Note that you can change the default Show When Inserting New Slides setting that displays the Slide Layout task pane whenever you insert new slides from the task pane.**

## Display and Hide the Slide Layout Task Pane

**①** Click **Format**.

**②** Click **Slide Layout**.

The Slide Layout Task pane appears.

*Note: You can also click **View**, and then click **Task Pane**, then click the **Other Task Panes** button and select **Slide Layout**.*

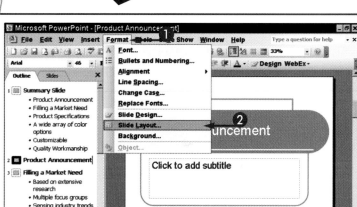

**③** Click the **Close** icon (⊠).

The Slide Layout Task pane closes.

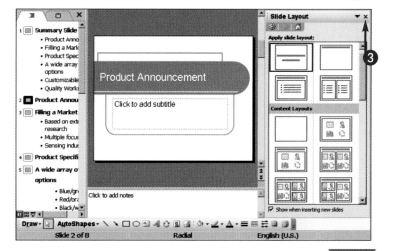

# Apply a Layout to a Single Slide

You can apply a layout to the currently displayed slide in Normal view or the currently selected slide in Slide Show view.

**You can also insert a new slide from the Slide Layout Task pane, which is covered in the section "Insert a New Slide with the Selected Layout."**

① Display the slide to which you want to apply the layout.

*Note: For more on starting a presentation, see Chapter 2.*

② Click **Format**.

③ Click **Slide Layout**.

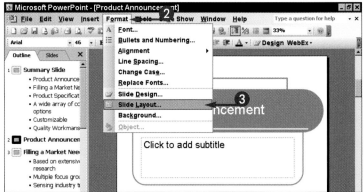

The Slide Layout Task pane appears.

④ Click a slide layout.

● The layout is applied to the slide.

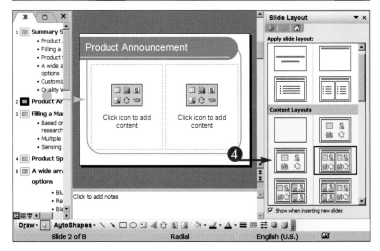

70

You can insert a new slide and then change its layout. But if you want a layout other than the default, you can save a step by applying the desired format when you insert the slide.

**Using the New toolbar button or the Insert command inserts the default slide layout automatically.**

## Insert a New Slide with the Selected Layout

1 Click the arrow (▮) on the right side of the layout you want in the Slide Layout task pane.

2 Click **Insert New Slide**.

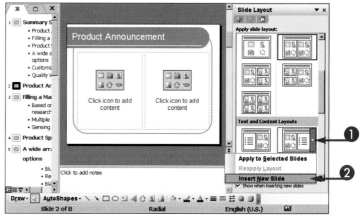

● A new slide with the selected layout appears.

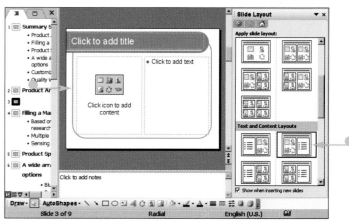

Content placeholders allow you to insert a variety of visual content.

### Clip Art

You can select an image from built-in clip art collections, or import a piece of clip art from outside PowerPoint.

### Pictures

Inserts a picture file such as a bitmap or JPEG you have stored on your computer or removable media, or downloaded from the Internet.

### Charts

Click to enter data that is then used to automatically generate a bar chart.

### Tables

Inserts a table and specify the number of rows and columns in it.

### Diagrams and Organizational Charts

Insert a diagram or organizational chart by choosing from a variety of types in a Diagram Gallery.

### Media Clips

Inserts sound or animation files from a Media Gallery or import a clip of your own.

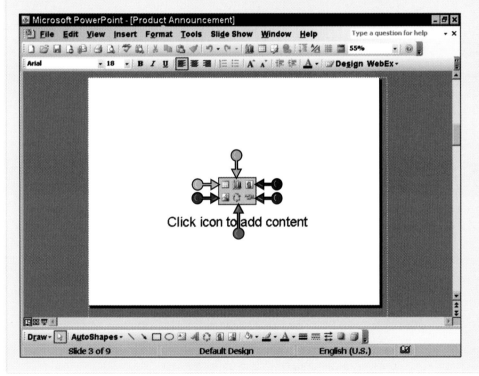

You can use diagrams to show a process or structure. For example, a diagram can show workflow in a procedure or the hierarchy in an organization.

**After you insert a diagram you can click it and type labels for various elements. You can use the Diagram toolbar that appears to make formatting changes.**

## Using Layouts with Diagrams

① With a slide containing a content placeholder, click the **Insert Diagram or Organization Chart** icon ([]).

The Diagram Gallery dialog box appears.

② Click a diagram type.

③ Click **OK**.

● The dialog box closes and the diagram appears on the slide ready for editing.

● A toolbar appears based on the type of diagram you selected.

● To edit the diagram you can double-click the element you want to modify.

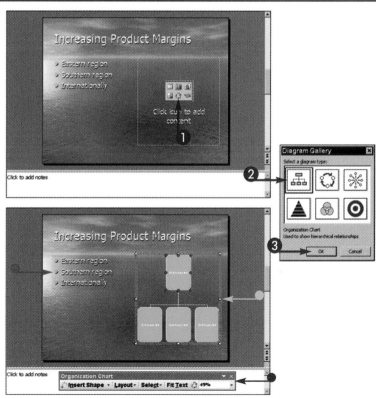

# Insert and Edit a Table

Tables allow you to organize information in rows and columns to easily show relationships among sets of data. For example, you might list regions of the country in the left column and several columns of data for sales by year for each region. You can insert a table with a content placeholder, and then type labels and data in the table cells.

## Insert and Edit a Table

### INSERT A TABLE

**①** With a content placeholder on a slide, click the **Insert Table** icon (▦).

The Insert Table dialog box appears.

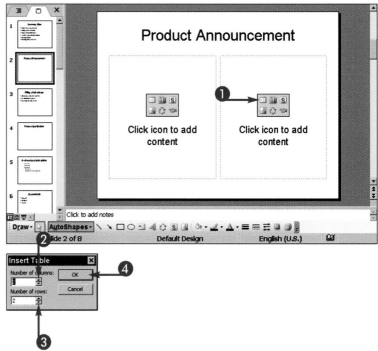

**②** Click here to set the number of columns.

**③** Click here to set the number of rows.

**④** Click **OK**.

**TYPE TEXT IN A TABLE**

A table appears ready for editing.

**5** Type a label or value in the first cell.

**6** Press **Tab**.

Your cursor moves to the next cell, and you can continue to type data.

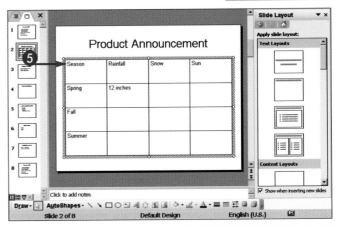

**7** Click outside the table.

The table appears on your slide.

● To make a change to the data in your table, you can click the content placeholder and it opens for editing.

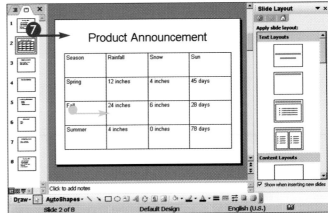

**TIPS**

**I originally created only three rows in my table, but now I find I need five. Can I add rows to tables?**

Yes. You can use the commands on the shortcut menu that appears when you right-click a table to insert rows. Click in the row above where you want to insert a row, right-click, and then click **Insert Row**. You can use a variation on this procedure to delete extra rows by right-clicking and selecting **Delete Row** from the shortcut menu that appears.

**Is there an easy way to format tables I create? For example, can I align text in the table cells or change the font?**

The best way to do this is to use the tools available on the Tables and Borders toolbar. Click **Tables and Borders** on the Standard toolbar to display the Tables and Borders toolbar. From there you can change the thickness of the table border, add fill color to cells, and align text within cells.

# Insert a Chart

Charts are a great way to present information in a visual way. They give an instant impression of trends or compared sets of data, such as sales growth over a several-year span. In PowerPoint, you can easily insert a simple bar chart by typing your data in a spreadsheet-like format.

## Insert a Chart

**INSERT THE CHART**

**1** With a slide containing a content placeholder displayed, click the **Insert Chart** icon (⚏).

A datasheet window appears filled with sample data and a sample chart is displayed.

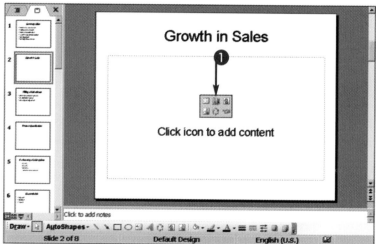

**2** Click in various cells to type column labels, row labels, and values.

**3** Click ✕.

The datasheet window closes and the chart appears open for editing.

To reopen the datasheet to edit data, you can right-click the chart and then click **Datasheet** from the menu that appears.

**CHANGE THE CHART TYPE**

④ Double-click the chart to open it for editing, if necessary.

● A border and handles appear around the chart.

⑤ Right-click the chart.

⑥ Click **Chart Type**.

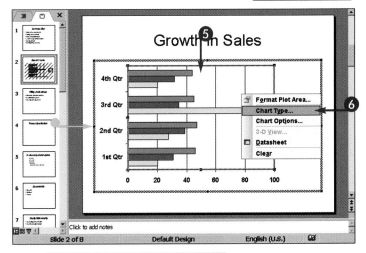

The Chart Type dialog box appears.

⑦ Click a chart type.

⑧ Click a chart sub-type.

⑨ Click **OK**.

The chart type changes.

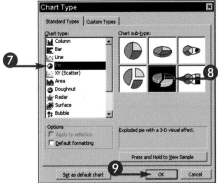

 **TIPS**

**Is there any way to format the elements in a chart?**

Yes. Double-click a chart to open it for editing. Right-click various elements in the chart, such as bars in a bar chart or the chart background area. In the shortcut menu that appears, select **Format**. The format options differ based on what you select. You can use the dialog box that appears to change formatting.

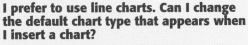

**I prefer to use line charts. Can I change the default chart type that appears when I insert a chart?**

Yes. Again, from the Chart Type dialog box, click the **Standard Types** tab. Next, click **Set as Default Chart**. When a message appears confirming that you want to make this setting, click **Yes**, and then click **OK**. Now PowerPoint uses the type of chart you selected whenever you insert a chart.

# Using Layouts with Pictures and Clip Art

You can easily insert pictures and clip art into your presentation for visual effect. Pictures might be photographs or scanned images in electronic form. Clip Art is a gallery of art of various types (photos, line drawings, and so on) that is included with PowerPoint.

Using Layouts with Pictures and Clip Art

## INSERT PICTURES

**1** With a slide containing a content placeholder displayed, click the **Insert Picture** icon (🖼).

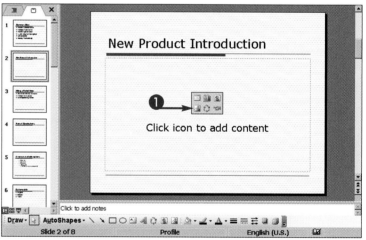

The Insert Picture dialog box appears.

**2** Click here and select a folder to look in.

**3** Click a file to open.

**4** Click **Insert**.

The selected picture is inserted into the placeholder.

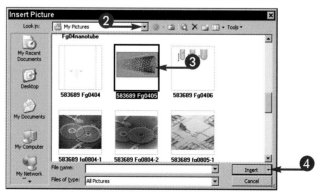

**INSERT CLIP ART**

1 With a slide containing a content placeholder displayed, click the **Insert Clip Art** icon ().

The Select Picture dialog box appears.

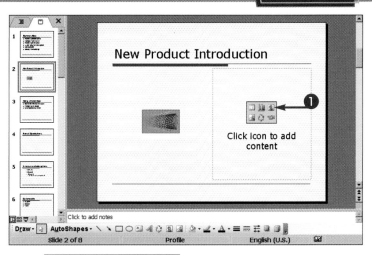

2 Type a term to search for a picture to fit your presentation.

This example uses the term **science**.

3 Click **Go**.

Pictures related to the search term appear.

4 Click a picture to select it.

5 Click **OK**.

PowerPoint inserts the selected picture into the placeholder.

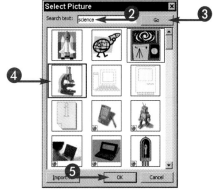

**TIPS**

**I use a picture for my soccer club logo all the time. Is there a way to add it to Clip Art?**

Yes. You can import the picture into the Clip Organizer. With the Select Picture dialog box open, click **Import**. Locate the picture on your hard drive or removable media, and click **Add**. The picture is now available through Clip Art.

**I see an Insert Picture icon (⊞) on the Picture toolbar. What does it do?**

It inserts a picture on the currently displayed slide, but the picture does not appear within a placeholder. If you click ⊞ in a content placeholder, the picture is inserted into the placeholder. Essentially, the effect is the same.

# Using Layouts with Media Clips

You can insert media clips into your presantation. Media clips are one type of Clip Art. They include both sound and animation clips that you can play automatically or manually during a presentation.

**You can also add your own sound or animation files to the Media Clip gallery using the Import button in the Media Clip dialog box.**

## Using Layouts with Media Clips

1 With a slide containing a content placeholder displayed, click the **Insert Media Clip** icon (🖳).

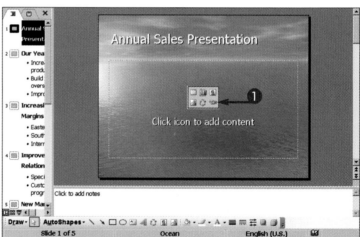

The Media Clip dialog box appears.

2 Type a term in the Search text field.

3 Click **Go**.

Associated clips appear.

4 Click a clip.

5 Click **OK**.

If you insert a sound clip, a dialog box appears asking how you want to start the media clip when you run a show.

- You can click **Automatically** to play the sound when the slide appears.

- Click **When Clicked** to play the sound when you click an icon.

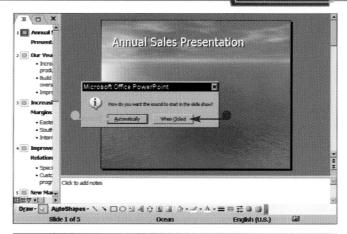

- An icon appears on the slide representing the clip.

*Note: What appears to represent the sound may vary depending on the sound file format.*

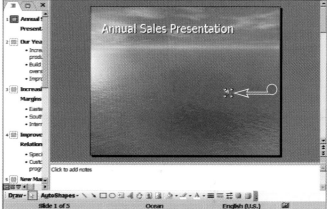

**TIPS**

**How can I tell which of the media clips are sounds and which are animations?**

Media clips are all lumped together when you search for one. Those with a little shooting star symbol (⊞) on the preview are animations. Those with no preview having a blue and red icon (⊡) are sound files.

**I have been searching by words but have not found what I want. Is there a way to just display all available clips at once?**

If you want to see all available media clips leave the search text box empty and click **Go**. All clips appear by default when you first open the Media Clip dialog box.

# Using Design Templates and Color Schemes

You can use PowerPoint's built-in templates to add professional-looking color and graphics to your presentations. Although you can apply slide backgrounds manually and add graphic elements one by one to design your slides, most people use PowerPoint's slide designs.

# Understanding Slide Designs

Slide designs are templates that include a variety of elements that make your slides look attractive.

## Slide Design Elements

Slide designs range from the blank background of the default design to designs that include all kinds of colors and graphics in the background. A slide design can include a background color (perhaps combined with a background graphic); graphic elements such as a picture or bars and lines; and fonts with their formatting settings, as well as positioning for all placeholders on slides.

## Apply Slide Designs

You can apply a slide design to a single slide, the entire presentation, or to selected slides in the same presentation. Generally it is better to use one slide design for an entire presentation so that the elements of all slides have a consistent look and feel. However, occasionally you might choose to combine two complementary slide designs for emphasis.

## Modify Slide Designs

Although slide designs are polished-looking combinations of elements that usually work just fine out of the box, you can put your own stamp on the design by modifying elements. You can, for example, change the background color or the entire color scheme. Changing the color scheme does not change fonts or graphic elements; it just changes the color used as the background to those elements.

## Slide Designs and Masters

Slide masters, which you can read more about in Chapter 7, are slides you can edit to add or delete graphic elements, and change the fonts used in the designs. In the slide master, for example, you find a title master and a slide master that you can modify to change the title slide as well as all other slides in your presentation. Changes made to slide designs in the Master view affect all slides because they are modifications to the template itself.

A slide design controls several aspects of your slides. For example, slide design determines where PowerPoint positions placeholders, the font and font size, the color scheme, and, in some cases, various graphic elements. To orient yourself to slide design, please note the various elements that a slide design controls.

**Positioning of placeholders**
Various placeholders, depending on the slide layout, are placed according to the slide design.

**Font and font size**
Slide design dictates font and font size for all text placeholders.

**Graphic elements**
Slide designs may or may not contain graphic elements. Some contain a background image such as clouds.

**Color**
The color scheme of a slide design controls the background color as well as the color of text and graphics.

You apply slide designs using the Slide Design task pane.

The Slide Design task pane includes three options you can display: Design Templates, Color Schemes, or Animation Schemes (these are covered in Chapter 10). By default, when you open the Slide Design task pane, it displays Design Templates with links to the Color or Animation Schemes.

**①** Click **Format**.

**②** Click **Slide Design**.

The Slide Design task pane appears.

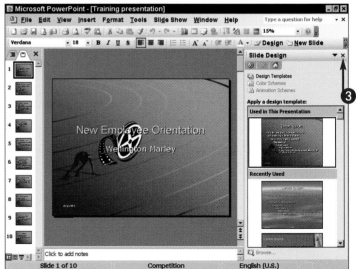

**③** Click the **Close** icon (⊠).

The task pane closes.

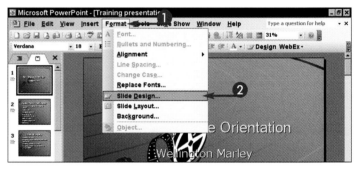

By default, new presentations have blank backgrounds for their slide designs, and they use the Arial font in varying sizes depending on the placeholder.

**Although it is easy to change designs at any time, you can make any slide design the default for every new presentation you start.**

### Make a Design the Default

① Click **Format**.

② Click **Slide Design**.

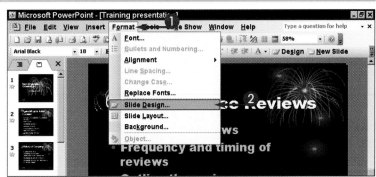

The Slide Design task pane appears.

③ Scroll to locate the Available for Use designs and locate the one you want.

④ Click the arrow on the side of the Slide Design preview.

⑤ Click **Use for All New Presentations**.

PowerPoint applies the design to the current presentation and to any new presentations you create.

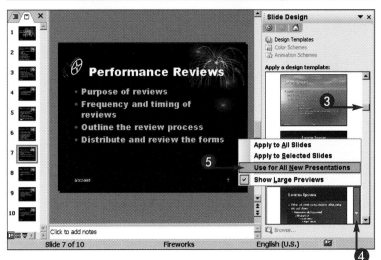

You can apply a slide design to the currently selected slide or slides in either Normal or Slide Sorter view. If you apply a different design to a single slide, be sure it complements the design used on other slides. The transition from one slide design to another as you move from slide to slide can be jarring to your viewers.

## Apply a Design to Selected Slides

① Click **Format**.

② Click **Slide Design**.

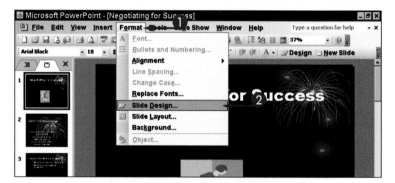

The Slide Design task pane appears.

③ To apply the design to more than one slide, select those slides in the Outline or Slide tab.

You can click a single slide or press and hold Ctrl as you click any other slides you want to format.

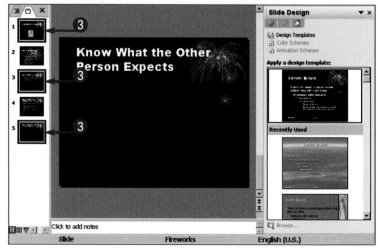

④ Scroll to locate the slide design you want to apply.

⑤ Click the arrow on the Slide Design preview.

⑥ Click **Apply to Selected Slides**.

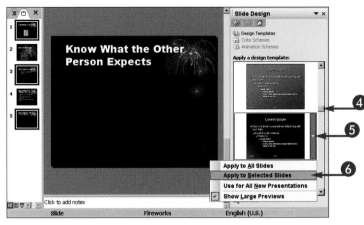

● The design is applied to the slides you selected.

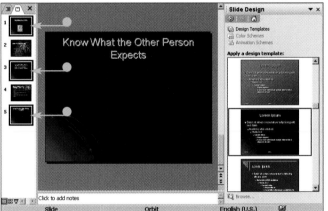

---

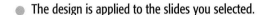

**If I change a few slides to use a different design template, can I use the master slide features for those slides?**

Yes. When you apply a design template to a presentation, you create a set of masters that have title and text. If you apply one template and then apply a different design template to one or more slides, you end up with two sets of masters that you can work with when you open the slide master. In Chapter 7, you learn the ins and outs of using masters.

**Do you have any advice for the kinds of templates that work best in presentations?**

Generally, darker backgrounds with light-colored text work better in a darker space, such as a hotel conference room. Lighter backgrounds are easier to read in a brighter, smaller space, such as a small meeting room. People may grow weary from looking at bright colors such as orange or red in longer presentations.

# Apply a Design to All Slides

The most common approach to slide design is to use a single look for your entire presentation. Slide designs vary the title slide look somewhat from other slide layouts, but retain an overall consistency for your presentation. See Chapter 5 for more about working with slide layouts.

① Click **Format**.

② Click **Slide Design**.

The Slide Design task pane appears.

③ Scroll to locate the slide design you want to apply.

④ Click the arrow on the side of the Slide Design preview.

⑤ Click **Apply to All Slides**.

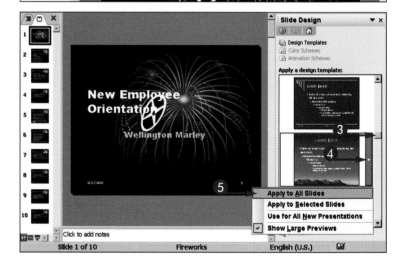

**6** Click the **Slide Sorter** icon (▦).

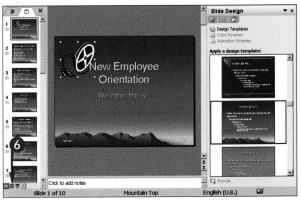

Slide Sorter view appears, showing that PowerPoint has applied the design to all slides.

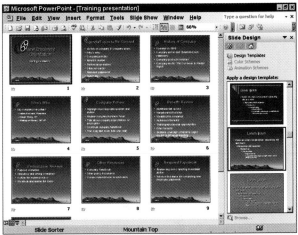

**When I click a design template preview, all my slides change. How do I change only a few of my slides?**

When you just click a design template preview, and do not use the preview menu to apply the template to selected slides you apply the template to all slides in the presentation. You must use click the arrow on the side of the Slide Design preview, shown in step **4**, and then click **Apply to Selected Slides**. This applies a design to only some slides in your presentation.

**One of the design templates is perfect for my presentation, but I want to add our soccer club logo to the slides. Can I do that?**

Yes. You can add any graphics or design elements to slides that you like. See Chapter 7 for information about masters, which allow you to add elements to all slides at once, and Chapter 8 for information about adding various graphic elements.

# Find Designs Online

PowerPoint comes with several built-in slide design templates, but sometimes you may want a change of pace. You can search for designs on the Internet by going to the Microsoft Office Online site, where templates are organized by categories such as Nature or Sports.

**When you download a template, you have to exit and relaunch PowerPoint, for the new design to appear in the Slide Design task pane ready to use with any presentation.**

## Find Designs Online

① With the Slide Design task pane open, scroll to the bottom of the list of template previews.

*Note: To open the Slide Design task pane, see the section "Apply a Design to All Slides."*

② Click the preview labeled **Design Templates on Microsoft Office Online**.

The Microsoft Office Online site opens in your browser.

*Note: You must have an Internet connection available to reach this site.*

③ Click a category link.

A list of templates appears.

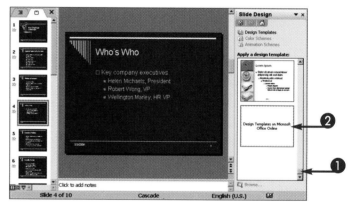

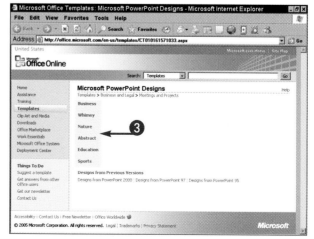

**4** Click a template.

A page with information about the template appears.

**5** Click **Download Now**.

*Note:* *A message may appear that says that an ActiveX control will be installed on your computer to manage downloads from the Microsoft Office Online site; click* ***Continue****.*

The template appears in PowerPoint in a new blank presentation with a Template Help task pane displayed.

The template is added to the top of the template list in the Slide Design task pane when you relaunch PowerPoint.

 **TIPS**

### I downloaded a template but now I do not like it. Is there a way to delete it?

Templates are stored on your computer's hard drive. Typically you find Office templates at c:\documents and setting\<your profile>\application data\Microsoft\templates. Use Windows Explorer to locate this templates folder, and then delete the file you no longer need.

### Does Microsoft offer any other sources for templates?

Yes. You can go to the Microsoft Office Marketplace at **www.office.microsoft.com/en-us/marketplace/**. There you can search Microsoft partners for templates, fonts, graphics, and more. These folks charge for their templates, but you may find just what you need. Some offer an unlimited download access price that may be worth it if you give a lot of presentations.

# Display and Close the Color Schemes Task Pane

When you open the Slide Design task pane it appears with the design templates list displayed. To work with the Color Schemes feature you must follow a link.

**Color schemes are displayed as thumbnails. You can use them to apply a scheme to one slide or all slides in your presentation.**

Display and Close the Color Schemes Task Pane

① Click **Format**.

② Click **Slide Design**.

The Slide Design task pane appears.

③ Click the **Color Schemes** link.

The Color Schemes list appears.

④ Click ☒.

The Task pane closes.

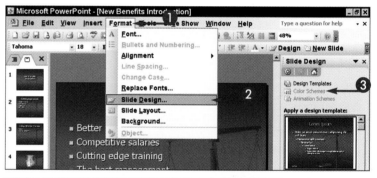

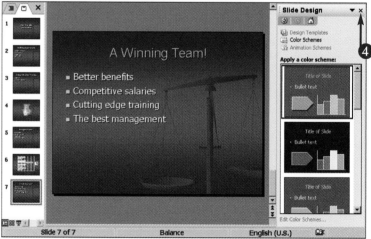

Typically you apply a single color scheme to your entire presentation for consistency. However, there may be times when you want a little more variety.

**You can select one or more slides in the Slide or Outline tab in Normal view, or in the Slide Sorter view. Then apply a color scheme to only the selected slides.**

## Apply a Color Scheme to a Slide

**①** Select the slides you want to change.

***Note:*** *To select multiple slides, you can click a slide and then press and hold* **Ctrl** *while clicking additional slides.*

**②** With the Color Schemes task pane open, click the arrow on a cd or scheme preview.

***Note:*** *To open the Color Schemes task pane, see the section "Display and Close the Color Schemes Task Pane."*

**③** Click **Apply to Selected Slides**.

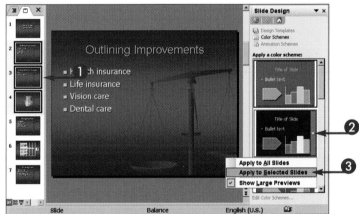

● The color scheme appears on selected slides.

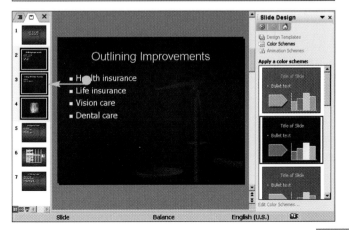

# Apply a Color Scheme to All Slides

Slide design templates come with a preset color scheme. However, you can change the color scheme for the entire presentation.

**Changing the color scheme can give a whole new look and feel to a design template, while retaining its other attributes.**

① With the Color Schemes task pane open, click the arrow on a color scheme preview.

**Note:** To open the Color Schemes task pane, see the section "Display and Close the Color Schemes Task Pane."

② Click **Apply to All Slides**.

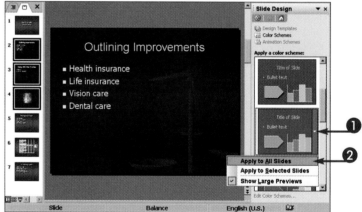

● PowerPoint applies the color scheme to the entire presentation.

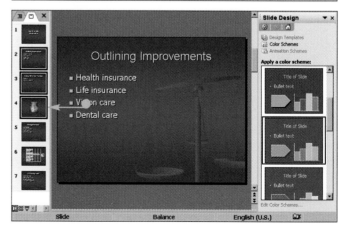

# Switch Between Previews

You can switch between larger and smaller previews. In both the Slide Design and Color Schemes task panes, PowerPoint shows you thumbnail previews of the various options.

**Smaller previews help you more quickly scroll through the available options, while larger previews help you see the details of a particular design or scheme.**

## Switch Between Previews

① In either the Slide Design or Color Schemes task pane, click the arrow on a preview.

**Note:** To open the Slide Design task pane, see the section "Apply a Design to All Slides." To open the Color Schemes task pane, see the section "Display and Close the Color Schemes Task Pane."

A menu appears.

② Click **Show Large Previews**.

PowerPoint inserts a check mark (☑) next to **Show Large Previews**.

If PowerPoint is displaying the default large previews when you perform step **2**, small previews now appear.

③ Click the arrow on a preview.

④ Click **Show Large Previews**.

PowerPoint inserts ☑ next to **Show Large Previews** and the large previews appear.

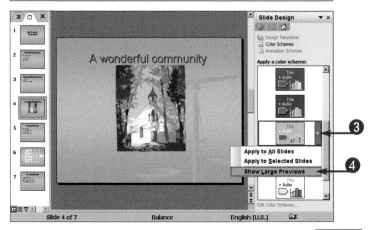

# Edit a Color Scheme

A color scheme consists of specified colors for the various elements that appear on slides. For example, the background may be one color, title text another, bullet point text and hyperlinks still another. You can edit and save a color scheme to create your own to use on other presentations.

## Edit a Color Scheme

**1** With the Color Schemes task pane open, click **Edit Color Schemes**.

*Note: To open the Color Schemes task pane, see the section "Display and Close the Color Schemes Task Pane."*

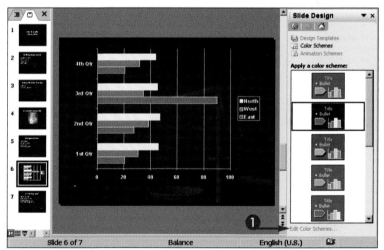

The Edit Color Scheme dialog box appears.

**2** Click a scheme element.

**3** Click **Change Color**.

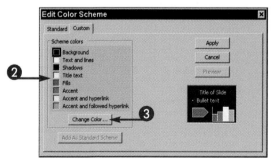

A Color dialog box appears.

④ Click the **Standard** tab, if necessary, to display it.

⑤ Click a color.

● A preview of the new color appears.

⑥ Click **OK**.

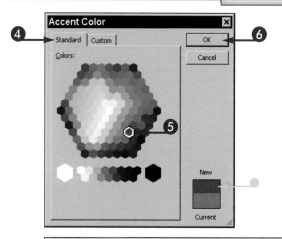

The change is made and the dialog box closes.

● To save this as a standard scheme without changing the original one, you can click **Add As Standard Scheme**.

⑦ Click **Apply**.

The dialog box closes and the changed scheme appears in the Color Schemes preview list.

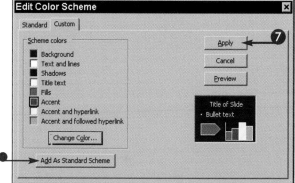

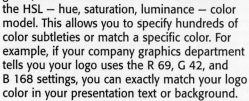
TIPS

**What is the Custom tab of the Color dialog box for?**

When you display the Color dialog box for an element, you can simply select from several dozen standard colors, or you can click the **Custom** tab to specify a color using the RGB — red, green, blue — color model or the HSL — hue, saturation, luminance — color model. This allows you to specify hundreds of color subtleties or match a specific color. For example, if your company graphics department tells you your logo uses the R 69, G 42, and B 168 settings, you can exactly match your logo color in your presentation text or background.

**I notice a background command on the Format menu. Is this the same as the background element you can change when editing a color scheme?**

Yes. The background command deals with the background color of slides as does the color scheme element. However, by using this dialog box you can change just the background without changing the color scheme or having to save a new standard color scheme. You also have additional tools through the **Background** menu command: You can make a setting that omits any graphics from the master slide on the currently selected slide; and you can add background fill patterns, in addition to changing the background color.

# Create Your Own Design Template

You can save a design template you have modified so that you can use it for future presentations. This saves you from having to re-apply these changes each time you want to use them. This involves saving the presentation in a template format.

**①** Click **File**.

**②** Click **Save As**.

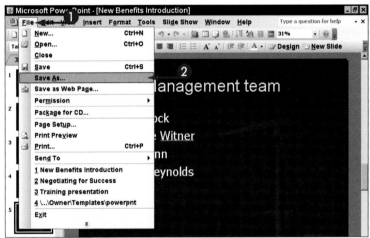

The Save As dialog box appears.

**③** Type a filename.

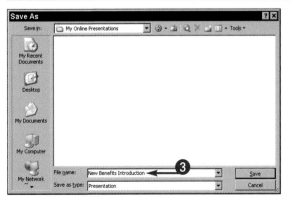

**4** Click here and select **Design Template**.

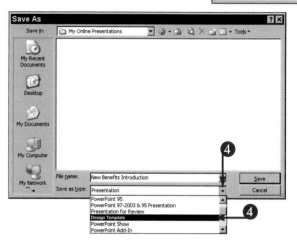

● The Save in folder changes to Templates.

**5** Click **Save**.

The presentation is saved as a design template and appears in the Design Templates preview list in the Slide Design task pane.

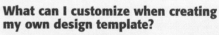

---

**TIPS**

**Some of the slide design templates on Microsoft Office Online are cool. Are there others out there?**

Yes. Lots of people and companies make PowerPoint templates available online. Some of them are free, and others will cost you. A few sites to explore are www.animationfactory.com and www.presentationcafe.com. Or type the term **PowerPoint templates** in your favorite search engine to find others.

**What can I customize when creating my own design template?**

You can use the Slide Master feature to make global changes to elements such as your background colors; graphic design elements, such as lines or borders; fonts; formatting; and graphics, such as pictures or clip art. Make all those changes first, and then save your file as a template.

# CHAPTER 7

# Using Masters

Masters allow you to make global settings for your slides, such as changing the font for the entire presentation or inserting your company logo on every slide.

# Understanding Masters

There are three master views available in PowerPoint. Each allows you to set up the basic infrastructure of your presentation to save you from making those settings on each and every slide.

## Work with Three Kinds of Masters

The three masters in PowerPoint are Slide Master, Handout Master, and Notes Master. Slide Master consists of a pair of items, a title master and a text master. They are related to the slides in your presentation and it is here that you set global text formats, bullet styles, and master graphics. Handout Master controls the layout of printed handouts; and Notes Master controls how printed notes pages look.

## Using Masters to Make Global Changes

When you make a setting, such as changing the font size for slide titles or adding a footer or graphic on a master, PowerPoint applies it to every slide in the presentation. This saves you time and gives your presentation a consistent look and feel.

## How Masters Relate to Slide Designs

When you apply a slide design to your presentation, PowerPoint automatically creates a set of slide masters containing all the settings of that slide design. If you go to Slide Master view and make changes, you can then preserve that master. If you apply more than one slide design to your presentation, you can create multiple master sets.

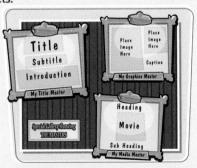

## Overriding Master Settings

When you make changes to individual slides, for example changing the font, that change takes precedence over master settings. You can also omit any graphics you have placed on Slide Master using the Background dialog box.

Slide Master view is where you make all settings for your slides. Slide Master view contains placeholders where you can set formatting for common text elements as well as various placeholders for footer information, date, and slide numbers.

### Title Master and Slide Master
These are the two masters created when you apply a slide design to your presentation.

### Slide Master View Toolbar
Use the tools on this toolbar to create, delete, preserve, or rename masters, or change the placeholders contained in the master layout.

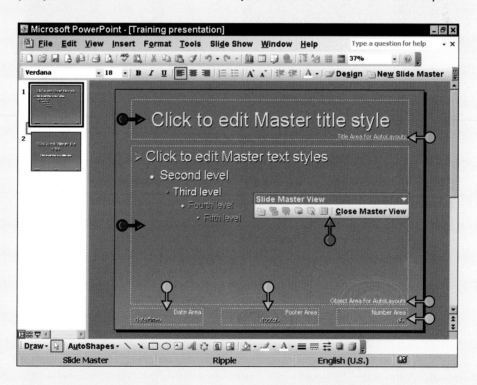

### Footer, Date, and Slide Numbers
Use these placeholders to add a date to every slide, set up slide numbering, or enter information, such as your company name, to every slide.

### AutoLayout Placeholders
You can select the text in these placeholders and apply formatting changes. These become the default text style for that placeholder on all slides.

# Display and Close Slide Master

Slide Master is essentially another view in PowerPoint, and you display it using the View menu. When you open Slide Master view, the Master toolbar is opened automatically.

**After you make your changes to Slide Master and close the view, you return to whatever view you had open when you went to Slide Master view – either Normal view or Slide Sorter view, where your global changes are reflected.**

## Display and Close Slide Master

① Click **View**.

② Click **Master**.

③ Click **Slide Master**.

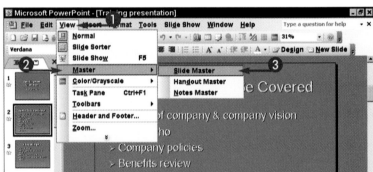

Slide Master view appears.

④ Click **Close Master View**.

Slide Master view closes.

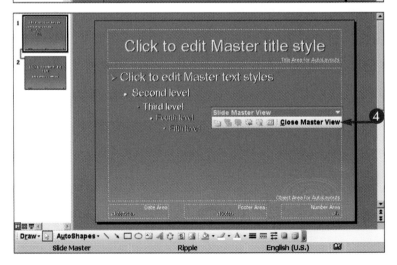

# Change the Slide Master Layout

By default, the Slide Master layout contains placeholders for the slide title, slide text, date, footer, and slide numbers. If you are not using a particular placeholder, you may find it distracting, and you may prefer to remove it from the master.

**You can delete any placeholder. When you do, you can then use the master layout feature to redisplay any of the default placeholders. Note that you can also resize or reposition any placeholder at any time.**

## Change the Slide Master Layout

**1** With Slide Master displayed, right-click the border of a placeholder.

A shortcut menu appears.

**2** Click **Cut**.

The placeholder disappears.

**3** Click the **Master Layout** icon (⊞) on the Master toolbar.

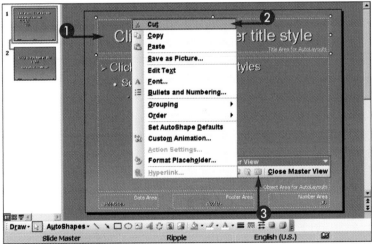

The Master Layout dialog box appears.

**4** Click the deleted item (☐ changes to ☑).

**5** Click **OK**.

The Master Layout dialog box closes and the placeholder reappears.

*Note: Any text you may have placed in the placeholder, such as the date, will be gone.*

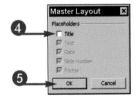

# Add a Footer

A footer is one of the placeholders that appears on all masters. Footers are useful for information you want to include on every slide, such as your company name or words such as "confidential" or "draft."

**If you enter text for your footer in the master views, PowerPoint includes it on all items of that type. For example, if you enter footer text in Handout Master, that footer appears on the bottom of a handout page, while a footer you enter in Slide Master appears on the bottom of each slide. You can also enter footer text in the Header and Footer dialog box.**

## Add a Footer

**1** With Slide Master displayed, click the master to which you want to add a footer.

**2** Click the footer area placeholder.

**3** Type footer text.

**4** Click **Close Master View**.

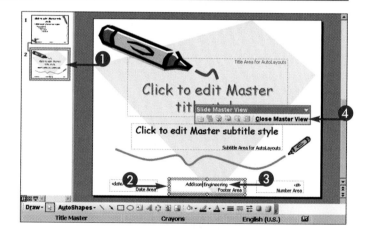

● The footer appears on every slide that matches that master type.

***Note:*** *You can control whether footers are displayed or not with the Header and Footer dialog box, which you open through the* ***View*** *menu.*

# Add a Date

You can enter a date in the date placeholder in a master; however that date is simply text and will not change with each presentation.

**To enter a date that is updated automatically based on your computer date, you have to make settings in the Header and Footer dialog box, which you can access from any view.**

## Add a Date

① Click **View**.

② Click **Header and Footer**.

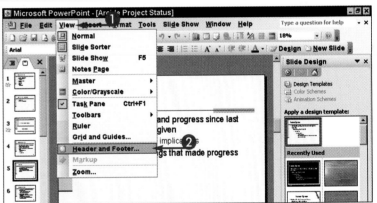

The Header and Footer dialog box appears.

③ Click **Date and Time** (☐ changes to ☑).

④ Click **Update Automatically** (◯ changes to ◉).

⑤ Click here and select a date or date and time style.

⑥ Click **Apply to All**.

PowerPoint adds the date to your master.

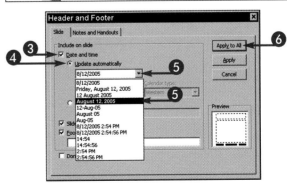

# Set Up Slide Numbers

Like the date, slide numbers that automatically increment for each subsequent slide in the presentation are set up in the Header and Footer dialog box.

**Although you can enter a number in the slide number placeholder in a master, that number will not automatically increment for each slide. Instead, use the master views to reposition or resize the slide number placeholder.**

## Set Up Slide Numbers

① Click **View**.

② Click **Header and Footer**.

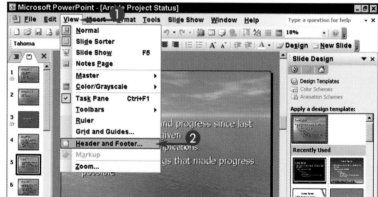

The Header and Footer dialog box appears.

③ Click **Slide Number** (☐ changes to ☑).

● The slide number placeholder appears in Preview.

④ Click **Apply to All**.

● You can click the **Close** icon (☒) to close the dialog box.

Slide numbers appear on all slides.

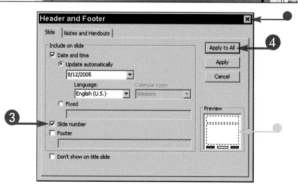

A very common use for the master views is to insert a graphic you want to appear on every slide. For example, you may want your company or organization logo to appear on each slide.

**When you insert a graphic on a master, you can reformat, resize, or reposition it just like any graphic that you place on a slide. See Chapter 8 for more about these procedures.**

## Insert a Graphic in Slide Master

**①** With Slide Master displayed, click **Insert**.

**②** Click **Picture**.

**③** Click **From File**.

*Note: You can also insert a graphic from any other source, such as Clip Art or WordArt. See Chapter 8 for more about these options.*

The Insert Picture dialog box appears.

**④** Click here and select the folder where the graphic is located.

**⑤** Click the graphic you want to insert into the master.

**⑥** Click **Insert**.

The dialog box closes and the picture is inserted on the master.

*Note: If you want to insert the picture on both title and text slides or on multiple masters, repeat this procedure on the other masters.*

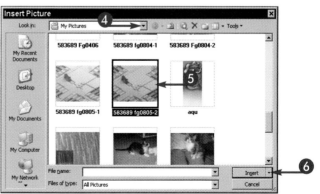

# Work with Multiple Masters

You may decide to use a few different looks in your presentation. For example, if you have one section in an HR presentation on benefits and another one on company policies, you may use a different slide design for each part.

## How Multiple Masters are Created

When you apply more than one slide design within a single presentation, you create multiple sets of masters. You can also create new masters from within Slide Master view, which use a design based on the default blank slide design. When you insert and format a new master in Slide Master view, that slide design is then available in the Slide Design task pane as a custom design.

## Manage Your Design with Multiple Masters

If you use different slide designs, make sure they are complementary. You can do this by selecting slide designs with similar color schemes, or similar designs such as Ripple and Ocean, which both use a water theme.

## Apply Additional Masters to Slides

When you have created multiple masters, you have to pick and choose which slides get which master applied. One easy way to do this is to select all the slides to which you want to apply one master, and then use the Apply to Selected Slides option on a slide design preview to apply it to only those slides.

## How and How Not to Use Multiple Masters

There are a few things to be cautious about when using multiple masters. First, do not use too many slide designs in one presentation or you get a cluttered, busy look that can distract viewers. Also remember that with multiple masters, changes you make on a master element only affect slides that have that one master applied, not all slides in the presentation. For changes you want on all slides, you have to do a little more work to apply them to multiple masters.

If you want to insert a custom master, you can do so in Slide Master view. Then you can use various methods to reformat text, change the background color, add graphics, and so on.

**Chapter 3 gives you procedures for formatting text, and Chapter 8 provides information on working with backgrounds and graphics. Using these methods you can create your own slide design from an inserted master.**

## Insert a New Master

① With Slide Master displayed, click **Insert New Slide Master** (🔲) on the Master toolbar.

● A new slide master appears in the list of masters.

The Insert New Title Master icon becomes available on the toolbar.

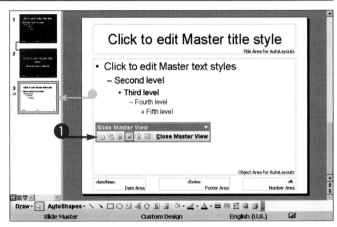

② Click **Insert New Title Master** (🔲).

● A new title master appears.

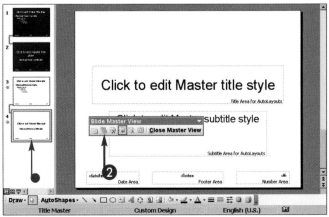

# Preserve a Master

Sometimes if you delete all the slides in a presentation that use a particular master, the master is deleted as well.

**To make sure that a master is not deleted, you should preserve it. Preserving one master of a pair of masters preserves both. Keep in mind, however, that even if it is preserved, you can still manually delete a master in Slide Master view.**

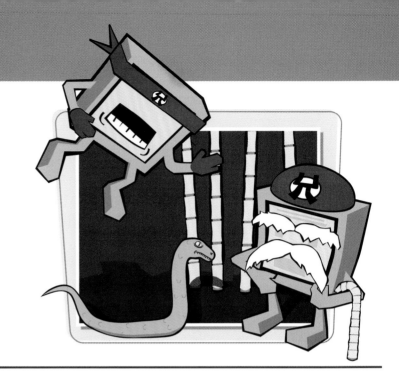

## Preserve a Master

**1** With Slide Master view displayed, click a master to select it.

**2** Click **Preserve Master** (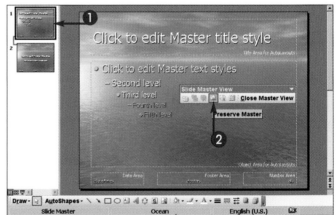).

● A pushpin symbol (⊞) appears next to the master in the list.

To unpreserve a master, perform steps **1** and **2** again.

If you insert a new master, it is named Custom Design in the Slide Design task pane. You may want to rename it to a more descriptive name. For example, a master that you apply a black background to and insert a graphic of a starburst on might be renamed Black Star.

On the other hand, if you apply a current slide design and make changes to it, you may choose to save it with a new name by renaming it. Then the original design and your customized design are both available to you.

## Rename a Master

① With the Slide Master displayed, click a master to select it.

② Click **Rename Master** (🖼).

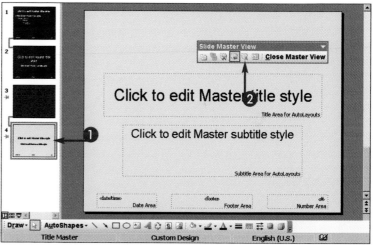

The Rename Master dialog box appears.

③ Type a name.

④ Click **Rename**.

The dialog box closes and the master is renamed.

If you press and hold your mouse over the master preview, the new name appears.

# Work with Notes Master

The Notes Master view is where you can modify the layout of the printed Notes format. Here you find a placeholder for slides, one for the Notes area, as well as header, footer, date, and slide number placeholders.

**You can modify the format of notes text, move placeholders around, delete placeholders, and enter header and footer text for printed Notes pages. See Chapter 12 for information about printing Notes.**

## Work with Notes Master

1 Click **View**.

2 Click **Master**.

3 Click **Notes Master**.

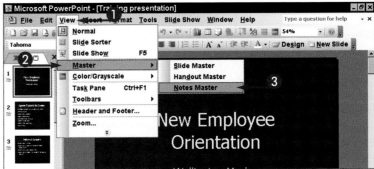

The Notes Master view appears.

4 Click and drag, or click and type elements that you want to add to your notes.

- You can select notes text and then click tools on the Formatting toolbar to change text formatting or font.

- You can click and drag a placeholder to another location on the slide.

- You can click and type to enter header text.

- You can click and type to enter footer text.

5 Right-click a placeholder.

A shortcut menu appears.

6 Click **Cut**.

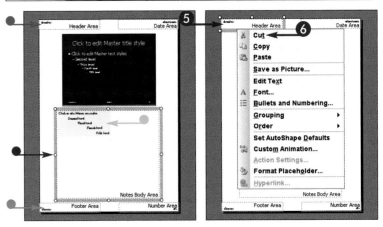

The placeholder disappears.

**7** Click **Notes Master Layout** ().

The Notes Master Layout dialog box appears.

**8** Click the omitted item (☐ changes to ☑).

**9** Click **OK**.

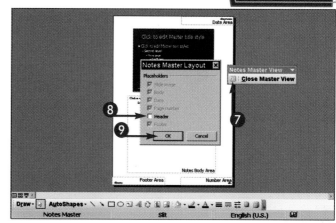

The placeholder is restored.

**10** Click **Close Master View**.

Notes Master view closes.

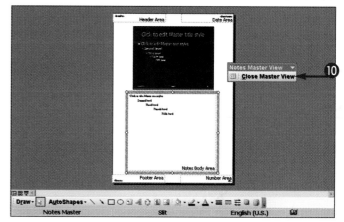

---

**TIPS**

**Is there a way to print just Notes, and not slides?**

Strangely, if you delete the slide placeholder from Notes Master view, the slide images still print on your Notes pages. One option is to click **File** and then click **Send** to send Notes and slides to Word. You can then delete the slide images in that document.

**How do I set the format for date and time to be printed on Notes?**

You can use the procedure for setting date and time for slides, but when you open the Header and Footer dialog box, click the **Notes and Handouts** tab. Then select the **Date and Time** option (☐ changes to ☑) and select a date and time format from the list. Click **Apply to All** and all your notes and handouts will use that date format.

# Work with Handout Master

In Handout Master view, you can look at various handout layouts and enter header and footer text to appear on printed handouts.

**Handout Master is perhaps the most limited in functionality of all the masters. You cannot change the position of the slides nor affect text formatting. You can simply enter header and footer text and reposition and resize header and footer placeholders, including date and slide number placeholders.**

## Work with Handout Master

### OPEN HANDOUT MASTER

1 Click **View**.

2 Click **Master**.

3 Click **Handout Master**.

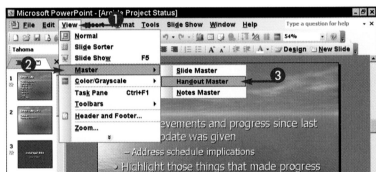

### DISPLAY A DIFFERENT LAYOUT

Handout Master View appears.

4 Click **Show Positioning of 9 per Page Handouts** (▦).

The preview changes to the new layout.

5 Click and drag the Footer Area placeholder to reposition it.

6 Click **Close Master View**.

Master view closes.

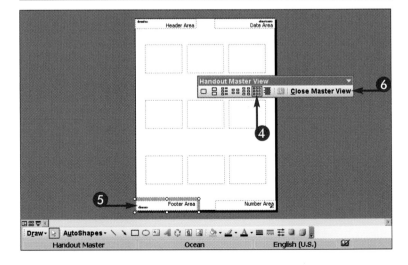

# Omit Master Graphics on a Slide

Although inserting a graphic on a title or slide master causes it to appear on every slide, you can override this on individual slides if you want. You might do this because the graphic overlaps other objects on a very full slide, for example.

**Omitting a master graphic is done using a setting in the Background dialog box. If you decide you want to display the graphic again at some point, you can simply repeat the steps provided below to reverse the setting.**

## Omit Master Graphics on a Slide

① In Normal view, click **Format**.

② Click **Background**.

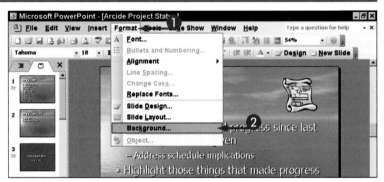

The Background dialog box appears.

③ Click **Omit Background Graphics from Master** (☐ changes to ☑).

Master graphics disappear from the preview.

④ Select one of two options:

● You can click **Apply** to omit the graphic from the current slide.

● You can click **Apply to All** to omit the graphic from all slides.

The Background dialog box closes and the master graphic is omitted.

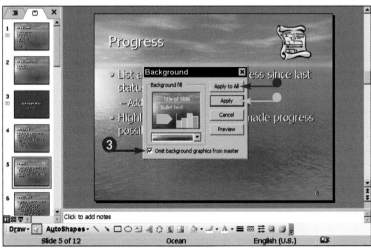

# Add Graphics and Drawings

Adding graphic elements such as photographs or clip art to your slides, and drawing various shapes can add visual interest to your presentation. You can also use color and various formatting options to get your presentation picture-perfect.

# Insert Clip Art

Clip art is a collection of picture, illustration, sound, and movie files. You can search for the image you want by using a keyword or phrase, and insert the image on your slide.

**There are built-in collections of clip art that come with Microsoft Office; you can also search free online collections of clip art if you have an Internet connection or buy clip art collections.**

Insert Clip Art

① With a slide displayed in Normal view, click **Insert**.

② Click **Picture**.

③ Click **Clip Art**.

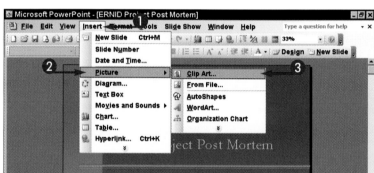

The Clip Art pane appears.

④ Type a search term.

⑤ Click the Results Should Be (⏷).

⑥ Click the check box next to an item to select (☐ changes to ☑) or to deselect (☑ changes to ☐) media types you do not need.

⑦ Click **Go**.

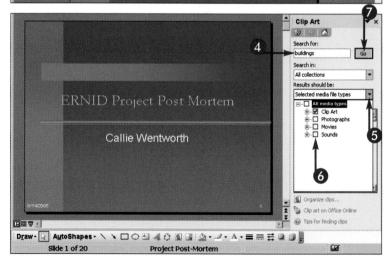

Search results appear.

**8** Scroll to locate the clip you want.

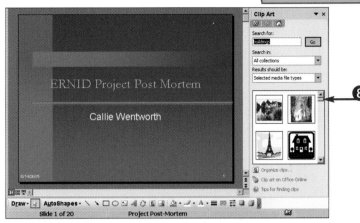

**9** Click the clip.

● The clip is inserted on your slide.

**I want to use Microsoft's online clips. How do I insert a clip from that collection?**

Before running your search in the Clip Art Task pane, click the Search In field ▼. Click the Web Collections item (☐ changes to ☑) to select it and click **Go**. PowerPoint will search online collections and include them in your search results.

**What happens if I insert a sound clip?**

When you insert a sound clip on a slide, a small megaphone icon appears on the slide. When you run a slide show, you can click that icon and the sound plays. You can also set up a sound to play automatically when the slide you insert it on appears during a slide show. See Chapter 10 for more about inserting sound and movie clips.

# Insert Images from Files

If you have image files stored on your computer, for example your company logo or a picture of your pet or house, you can insert those images onto your PowerPoint slides.

**After you insert an image file, it becomes an object on your slide that you can move around, resize, and even format. See the section "Edit Pictures" for information about formatting picture files.**

## Insert Images from Files

**①** Display the slide you want to insert the image on in Normal view.

**Note:** *For more on Normal view, see Chapter 1.*

**②** Click the **Insert Picture** icon (![icon]).

● You can also click **Insert**, **Picture**, **From File** to open this dialog box.

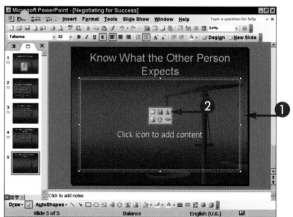

The Insert Picture dialog box appears.

**③** Click here and select the folder where the image is located.

**④** Click the image file you want to insert.

**⑤** Click **Insert**.

● The image appears on your slide.

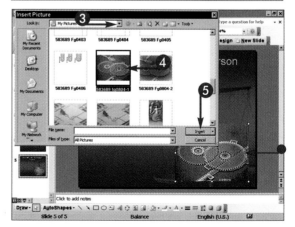

AutoShapes are drawing tools that help you draw more complex shapes such as stars or arrows with a simple click and drag action.

**AutoShapes also enable you to draw callout balloons, squiggly lines, and connector lines that are useful in creating flow charts. After you draw an AutoShape you can apply various formats to it. See the section "Format Objects" for more about how this is done.**

## Draw AutoShapes

① With the slide you want to insert an AutoShape in displayed in Normal view, click **AutoShapes** on the Drawing toolbar.

② Click a category, such as **Stars and Banners**.

③ Click a style of AutoShape, such as **4-Point Star**.

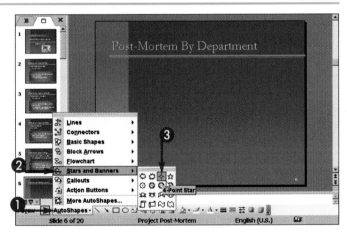

The AutoShape menu disappears and your mouse cursor turns into the shape of a plus sign.

④ Click and drag on your slide where you want the AutoShape to appear.

⑤ Release your mouse.

The AutoShape is drawn.

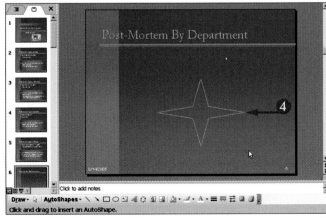

# Draw Objects

If you want to draw simple shapes such as circles or squares, you can use tools on the Drawing menu. These shapes, the Oval, Rectangle, Line, and Arrow tools, are actually AutoShapes accessible from the Drawing toolbar.

**You can click and drag to draw a symmetrical object, such as a circle, or asymmetrical, such as an oval. You can move and resize a drawn object. See the section "Move and Resize Objects" for more about how to do this.**

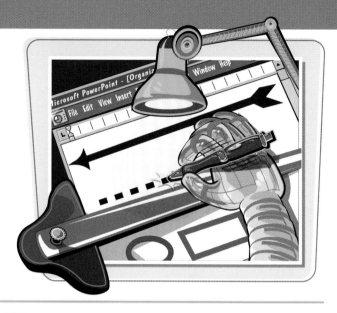

**①** With the slide on which you want to draw an object displayed in Normal view, click the **Oval tool** icon (⬭).

*Note: See Chapter 1 for more on Normal view.*

Your mouse cursor changes to the shape of a plus sign.

**②** Click and drag on your slide.

The object is drawn.

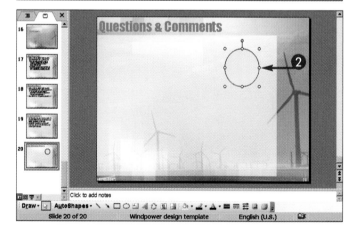

You can enter text in any drawing object. However, a text box is a drawing object that automatically enlarges or shrinks depending on the amount of text you type and includes a text wrap feature that places text on consecutive lines.

**Text you type in a text box does not appear in your presentation outline. Because of this, you may want to use a text box as more of a design feature.**

## Add a Text Box

1 With the slide you want to add a text box to displayed in Normal view, click the **Text Box** icon (⬚) on the Drawing toolbar.

Your mouse cursor changes to the shape of an upside-down cross.

2 Click and drag on your slide.

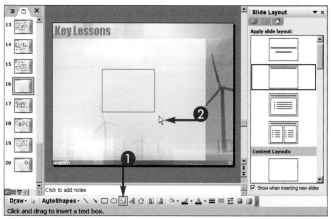

The text box appears, open for editing.

3 Type your text.

4 Click anywhere outside the text box.

The text appears on your slide.

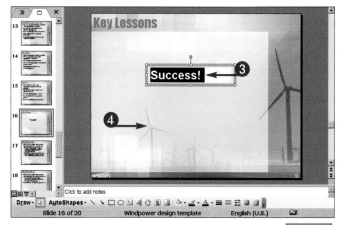

# Format Objects

Drawing objects, including AutoShapes and ovals, rectangles, lines, and text boxes, can all be formatted in a variety of ways. For example, you can add a fill color, change the thickness or color of the lines that define the shape of the object, and modify arrow styles. Changing object formatting can add visual appeal and make the object easier to see against the background of your slide.

**When filling an object with color or changing line colors, try to pick colors that complement your presentation's color scheme. You can group together several formatted drawing objects to create an illustration, such as a flower. See the section "Group and Ungroup Objects" for more about this feature.**

### Format Objects

❶ Right-click a drawing object on your slide.

❷ Click **Format AutoShape**.

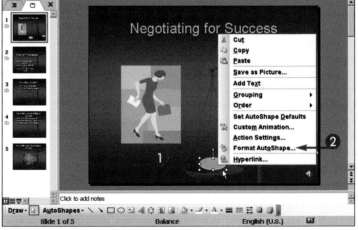

The Format AutoShape dialog box appears.

❸ Click here for Fill Color to format the interior of the object or Line Color to format the outside line of the object.

A color palette appears.

❹ Click a color you want to fill the object with or apply to a line.

❺ Click and drag to make the object fill more or less transparent.

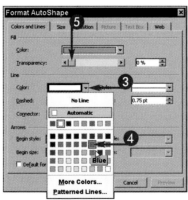

**6** Click here and select a dashed line from the list.

**7** Click here and select a style to apply it.

● If you selected a line or arrow object, you can also use the Arrows fields to change the beginning and ending arrow styles.

**8** Click **OK**.

PowerPoint applies the formatting changes.

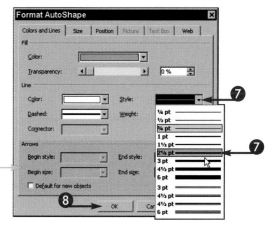

**TIPS**

**I want to have all the AutoShapes I draw appear with a blue fill color. Is there a quick way to do that?**

Yes. In the Format AutoShape dialog box, select the color of blue that you want from the color palette. Then click the **Default for New Objects** option (☐ changes to ☑) and click **OK**. Now when you draw objects, they all fill with blue.

**Can I use some sort of fill pattern for my objects?**

Yes. At the bottom of the Fill color palette in the Format AutoShapes dialog box, click **Fill Effects**. This displays a dialog box that allows you to apply various effects to your AutoShapes, including fill patterns such as stripes or diamonds, gradients — seeming variations in light — textures such as marble or water drops, or even pictures.

# Move and Resize Objects

When you draw an object or insert a picture, it may not appear in the place or at the size you prefer. In that case you can resize the object to fit better on your slide, and move it wherever you want.

**You resize objects using handles; small squares that surround the object when it is selected. You can drag these handles to make an object larger or smaller. Dragging on corner handles retains the object's original proportions; dragging any other handle distorts the original proportions, so that, for example, a square may turn into a rectangle.**

Move and Resize Objects

## MOVE OBJECTS

**1** Click an object to select it.

Your mouse cursor changes to four overlapping arrows when you hold it over the selected object.

**2** Drag the object to a new position.

**3** Release the mouse.

● The object appears in its new position.

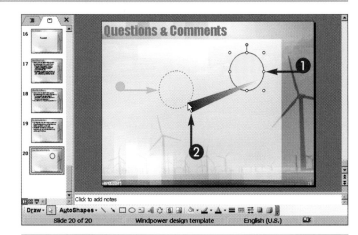

## RESIZE OBJECTS

**1** Click an object to select it.

Handles appear around it.

**2** Click a handle and drag outward to enlarge it or inward to shrink it.

**3** Release the mouse.

The object is resized.

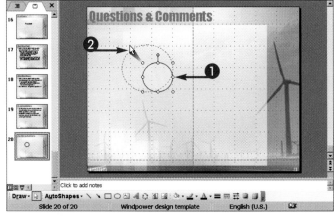

Sometimes to create an illustration with several drawing objects, or to better fit an object on a slide, you must rotate it. PowerPoint allows you to rotate an object 360 degrees, or use a Flip feature to quickly flip it from left to right or right to left.

**You can use the Drawing menu to flip an object or to rotate it 90 degrees. You can also use a click and drag method to freely rotate an object 360 degrees using rotation handles.**

## Rotate and Flip Objects

### ROTATE OBJECTS

① Click an object.

Handles appear around it, including a green rotation handle.

② Click the rotation handle and drag it to the left or right.

The object spins.

③ Release the mouse.

The object is rotated.

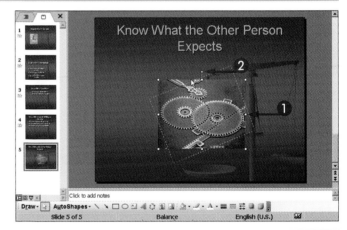

### FLIP OBJECTS

① Click an object to select it.

② Click **Draw**.

③ Click **Rotate or Flip**.

④ Click **Flip Horizontal** or **Flip Vertical**.

The object is flipped 180 degrees in the selected direction.

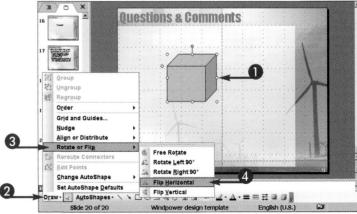

WordArt is a little application that comes with Microsoft Office that allows you to create 3D-type text effects. Using WordArt you can create text in a circle, or text that appears to be stretched. You can use WordArt to place emphasis on a very important word or phrase, or to design a simple logo, for example.

**You can move or resize a WordArt object, change its color, or rotate it. See the sections "Move and Resize Objects," "Format Objects," and "Rotate and Flip Objects" for more information.**

## Add WordArt

**1** With the slide on which you want to insert WordArt displayed in Normal view, click **Insert**.

*Note: For more on Normal view, see Chapter 1.*

**2** Click **Picture**.

**3** Click **WordArt**.

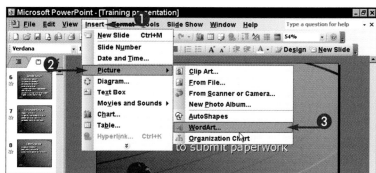

The WordArt Gallery appears.

**4** Click a WordArt style.

**5** Click **OK**.

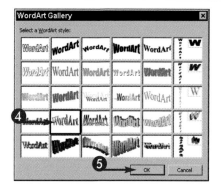

The Edit WordArt Text dialog box appears.

⑥ Type a word or words.

⑦ Click here and select a font from the list that appears.

⑧ Click here and select a font size.

⑨ Click **OK**.

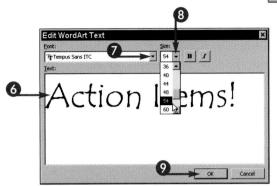

● The WordArt object appears on the slide.

● The WordArt toolbar appears.

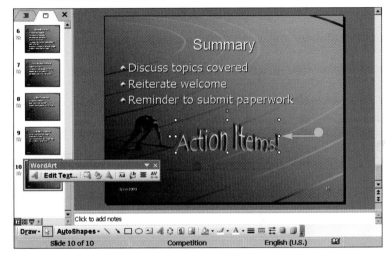

**I created a WordArt object, but then realized it contains a typo. Is there any way to change it?**

Yes. Double-click the object and the Edit WordArt Text dialog box opens. Edit or replace the existing text, and click **OK**. The new WordArt object displays. You can also use this method to change the font, font size, or add bold or italic effects to the WordArt.

**I want to change the style and color of the WordArt. What is the best way to do that?**

When you click a WordArt object, the WordArt toolbar appears. Click the **WordArt Gallery** icon (🔲) to display the various WordArt styles and select another one. You can click the **Format WordArt** icon (🔲) to open the Format WordArt dialog box and edit the colors used in the fill and line for the WordArt object.

# Edit
# Pictures

When you insert a graphic file, whether it is one of your own or a piece of clip art, you can edit it using the Picture toolbar. You can adjust the color and modify the contrast and brightness to make the image crisper.

**You can also rotate the image, or crop it to get rid of portions you do not need to show. The Picture toolbar also allows you to add a line border around the picture, or recolor it. Note that you can only recolor WMF – Windows Media Files, such as some of the illustrations you find in clip art – but not photographs.**

Edit Pictures

## DISPLAY THE PICTURE TOOLBAR

**1** Insert a picture object on a slide.

*Note: To insert a picture object, see the section "Insert Clip Art."*

**2** Click the picture.

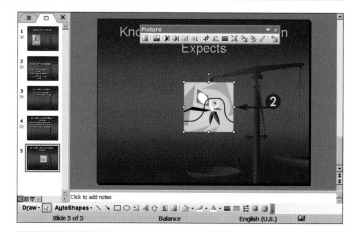

## MODIFY IMAGE QUALITY AND ADD A BORDER

The Picture toolbar appears.

**3** Click any of the following tools to adjust the image quality:

● You can either click the **More Contrast** icon (■) to make darks and lights more distinct or the **Less Contrast** icon (■) to make darks and lights less distinct.

● You can either click the **More Brightness** icon (■) to lighten the picture or the **Less Brightness** icon (■) to darken the picture.

**4** Click the **Line Style** icon (≡).

**5** Click a style.

A border is applied using that style.

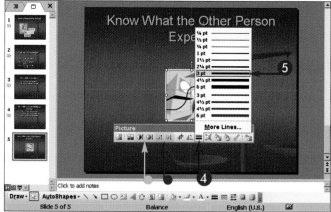

## CROP THE PICTURE

1 Click the **Crop** icon ( ).

● Corner and side markers appear around the picture and your cursor changes to a cropping tool when you hold it over these markers.

2 Click a marker and drag inward to remove an edge of the picture.

3 Click  again to turn the tool off.

## RECOLOR A PICTURE

1 Click the **Recolor Picture** icon ( ).

The Recolor Picture dialog box appears.

*Note: This does not work with bitmap files. Use a clip art illustration for these steps.*

2 Click an item in the Original column ( changes to ).

3 On the corresponding New item, click here and select a new color.

● The preview reflects the new color.

4 Repeat steps **2** and **3** for other original items.

5 Click **OK**.

The new colors are applied.

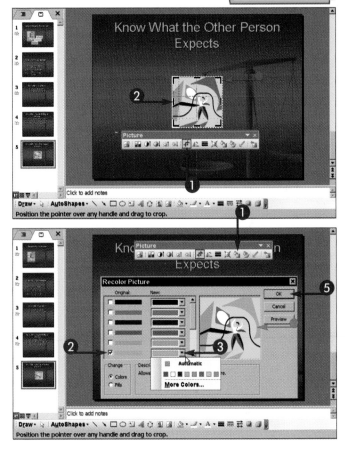

 **TIPS**

**There is a tool called Compress Picture on the Picture toolbar. What does it do?**

Image files can get very large. When you insert them into your presentation, your PowerPoint file itself can become quite large. This may slow down PowerPoint's performance when you give a presentation. One way to make your file smaller is to compress picture files. This takes out redundant or unnecessary data without having a great impact on image quality.

**I click a picture but the Picture toolbar does not appear. What can I do to display it?**

This usually happens if you select the picture, and then close the Picture toolbar. If you click the picture again the toolbar does not redisplay. You can click **View**, **Toolbar**, and then **Picture** to display the toolbar. Or right-click the picture and click **Show Picture Toolbar** from the shortcut menu that appears.

# Group and Ungroup Objects

You may create a set of objects that you want to move around your slide as a unit. For example, you may use ovals and lines to create a drawing of a car or house. To treat a collection of drawings, photos, or other objects as a single object, you have to group them.

**When grouped, you can move the objects, rotate them, format, or resize them as one object. To work with the individual objects again you have to ungroup them. You group and ungroup objects using a command in the Draw menu.**

Group Objects

## GROUP OBJECTS

① Click an object.

The object is selected.

② Press **Ctrl** and click one or more other objects.

③ Click **Draw** on the Drawing toolbar.

④ Click **Group**.

## UNGROUP OBJECTS

● A single set of handles appears around the grouped object.

⑤ Click the grouped object.

⑥ Click **Draw**.

⑦ Click **Ungroup**.

The objects are once again separate.

# Change Object Order

When you work with object, sometimes you want to stack them in layers, like a fanned out deck of cards. When you do this, you have to set up which object is on top of the stack and which objects are underneath. This is the object order setting.

**The commands you can use to change order allow you to bring an object in front of any other objects in the stack, or all the way to the back. You can also choose to bring an object forward or backward one layer at a time.**

## Change Object Order

**1** With several objects overlapping on your slide, click an object lower in the stack.

**2** Click **Draw**.

**3** Click **Order**.

**4** Click **Bring to Front**.

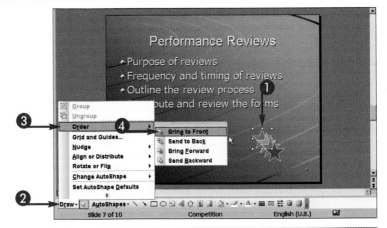

The object is placed at the top of the stack.

**5** Click **Draw**.

**6** Click **Order**.

**7** Click **Send to Back**.

● The object moves to the bottom of the stack.

● To send the object forward only one layer, click **Bring Forward;** to send the object back only one layer, click **Send Backward**.

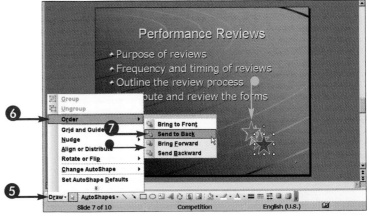

# Using the Grid and Guides

There are two features of PowerPoint that help you position objects and placeholders on a slide more exactly. The grid is like the lines on graph paper displayed on your slide. You display the grid and use it to place items at a regular distance from each other.

Guides, on the other hand, are two intersecting lines that you can move like rulers around your slide. You use guides to place an item at the exact spot where the guides intersect.

## Using the Grid and Guides

**TURN ON THE GRID AND GUIDES**

① Click **View**.

② Click **Grid and Guides**.

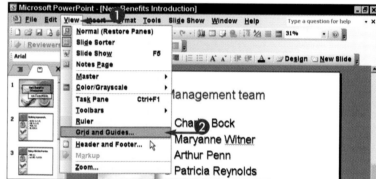

The Grid and Guides dialog box appears.

③ Click the **Display grid on screen** option (☐ changes to ☑).

④ Click the **Display drawing guides on screen** option (☐ changes to ☑).

⑤ Click **OK**.

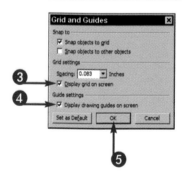

● The grid appears as dotted lines.

● The dashed line guides intersect in the center of the slide.

⑥ Click and drag an object to line it up with the grid.

⑦ Click and drag another object to line it up with the first one using the grid as a guide.

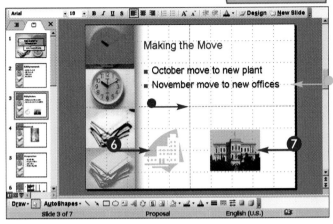

⑧ Click a guide line.

● Numbers representing the position of the guide appear showing the new intersection of the two guides.

● You can click and drag any object into a specific position on the slides at the intersection of the guides.

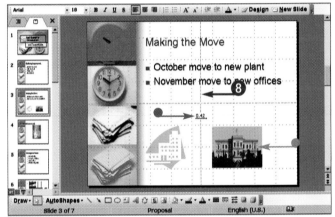

**TIPS**

**Is there a way to get objects to automatically line up along grid lines?**

Yes. You can use the Snap to feature. Open the Grid and Guides dialog box. Click the **Snap Objects to Grid** option (☐ changes to ☑). Click **OK**. Now when you move an object around the slide, if it is close to a grid line, it snaps into position with it. This helps you automatically align things on your slide.

**It would be helpful to me to have a smaller network of grid lines. How do I do that?**

Once again in the Grid and Guides dialog box, you can modify the spacing between grid lines, forming larger or smaller boxes. Under Grid Settings, click the Spacing ▾ and select a different measurement from the list. Click **OK**, and the new spacing is set.

# Nudge Objects

It is often tricky to move an object by very small increments on a slide. A drawing feature called Nudge helps in this situation. Nudge allows you to move a selected object one pixel to the right, left, up, or down on the slide.

**There is also a shortcut keystroke combination you can use to nudge an object on a slide. Either of these methods helps line things up on a slide more easily.**

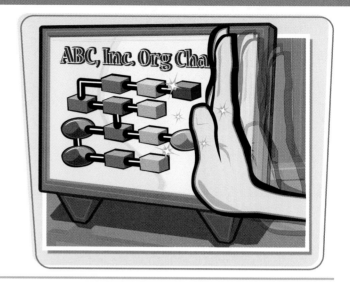

① Click an object to select it.

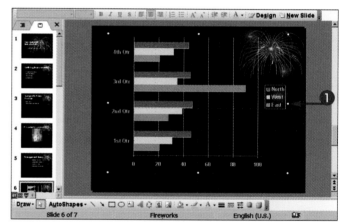

② Click **Draw**.

③ Click **Nudge**.

④ Click either **Up**, **Down**, **Left**, or **Right**.

You can also press Ctrl and then press ↓, ←, →, ↑ to nudge an object in a specific direction.

The object moves one pixel in that direction.

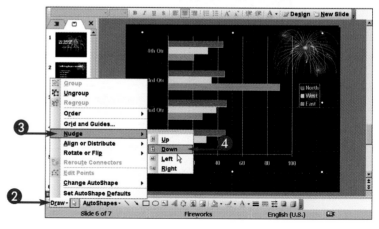

You can align objects relative to each other or relative to the edge of a slide. For example, you can place a picture at the exact center of the slide, or align one object along the top and one along the bottom.

**The Align or Distribute command on the Draw menu allows you to align objects or to distribute them equally across a slide, either horizontally or vertically.**

## Align Objects

### ALIGN OBJECTS

1 Click an object.

2 Press **Ctrl** and click one or more other objects.

3 Click **Draw**.

4 Click **Align or Distribute**.

5 Click any one of the six Align commands.

The object is aligned.

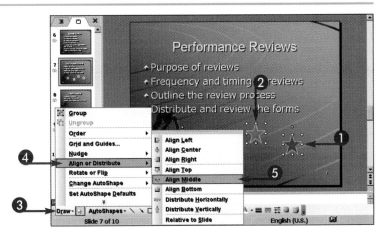

### DISTRIBUTE OBJECTS

1 Click an object.

2 Press **Ctrl** and click another two or more objects.

3 Click **Draw**.

4 Click **Align or Distribute**.

5 Click **Distribute Horizontally** or **Distribute Vertically**.

The objects are distributed accordingly.

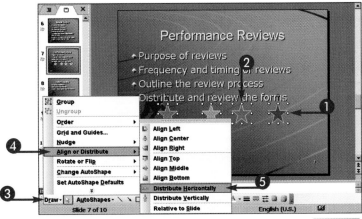

# Organize Slides

After you have created several slides, you need to be sure that the overall flow of your presentation makes sense. The best place to organize your slides is in Slide Sorter view. This view gives you thumbnails, which are little pictures, of all your slides so you can easily move them around, or delete or add duplicate slides.

To build a presentation you must create a sequence of ideas that leads your viewer in a logical progression. When creating a presentation, you often have to reorganize slides to get that sequence just right.

**You may also want to rearrange slides to create variations on an original presentation that places the emphasis on different ideas.**

① If you are not in Slide Sorter view, click **Slide Sorter** (▦).

The Slide Sorter view appears.

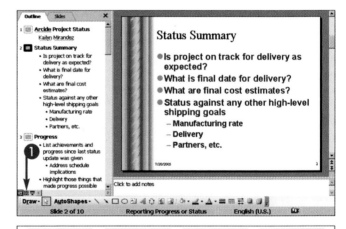

② Click and drag a slide.

● A line appears to indicate the new slide position.

③ Release the mouse button.

The slide appears in its new position.

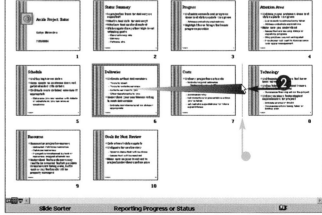

After you have created several presentations, you may decide you want to copy a slide from one presentation to another. In this case you can simply copy and paste the slide.

**If you want to copy a slide within the same presentation you can use the Duplicate Slide feature, which saves a few steps. See the section "Make a Duplicate Slide" later in this chapter for more information.**

## Copy and Paste a Slide

1. With a PowerPoint presentation open in Slide Sorter view, click the slide you want to copy.

2. Click **Edit**.

3. Click **Copy**.

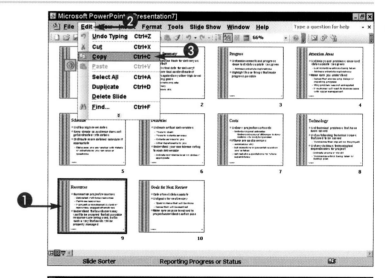

4. Open another presentation.

*Note: For help with opening presentations, see Chapter 2.*

5. In any view or pane, click the slide you want the copied slide to appear after.

6. Click **Edit**.

7. Click **Paste**.

   The copy of the slide is pasted into this presentation.

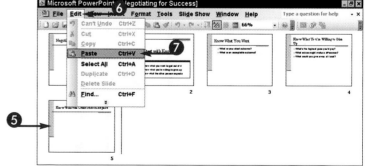

# Delete a Slide in Slide Sorter View

As you build your presentation you may decide you do not need a particular topic. In this case you can simply delete that slide.

**It is common to build one presentation and then use it as the basis for other presentations. In this case you may also need to delete several slides that are irrelevant or out of date.**

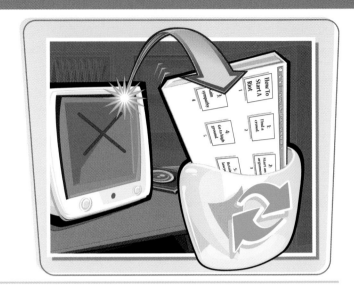

## Delete a Slide in Slide Sorter View

① With a PowerPoint presentation open in Slide Sorter view, click the slide you want to delete.

You can press **Ctrl** and click several slides to select more than one slide to delete at a time.

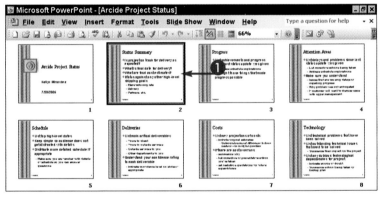

② Click **Edit**.

③ Click **Delete Slide**.

The slide is deleted from the presentation.

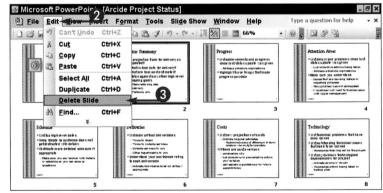

If you are reorganizing many slides, you may simply want to see the slide titles and not the more detailed content. In this case you can hide the formatting in Slide Show view.

**When you hide formatting, everything but the slide titles disappears, including slide design and background elements.**

## Hide Formatting

① With a presentation displayed in Slide Sorter view, click **Show Formatting** (⧄).

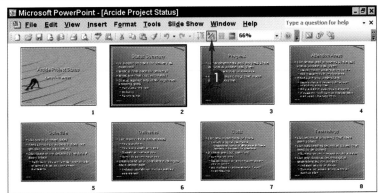

All formatting disappears.

② Click ⧄.

The formatting reappears.

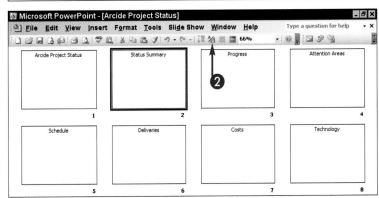

# Make a
# Duplicate Slide

Some things bear repeating, which is why you may want to duplicate a slide. When you do, you can use the Duplicate Slide feature.

**A common use of the Duplicate Slide feature is to make a second copy of a summary slide so you can have one at the beginning and end of a presentation. See the section "Insert a Summary Slide" later in this chapter for more on summary slides.**

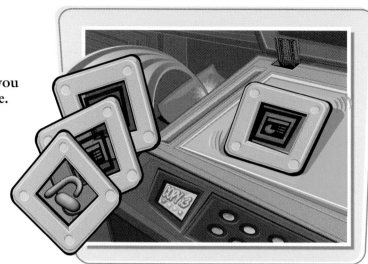

## Make a Duplicate Slide

**1** With a PowerPoint presentation open in Slide Sorter view, click the slide you want to duplicate.

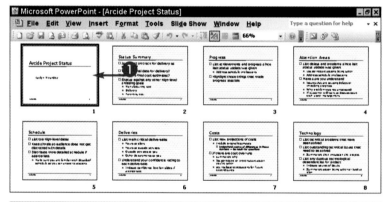

**2** Click **Edit**.

**3** Click **Duplicate**.

A copy of the slide is pasted to the right of the currently selected slide.

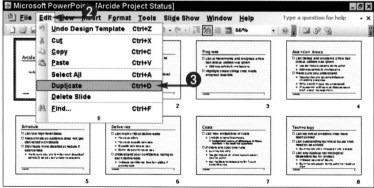

Hiding a slide allows you to create
mini-presentations from a master presentation.
Instead of deleting slides you can hide them,
give the presentation, and then unhide them.

**You may also want to hide a few
slides temporarily to see how your
presentation flows without them.**

## Hide a Slide

**1** With a PowerPoint presentation open in Slide
Sorter view, click the slide you want to hide.

You can press **Ctrl** and click to select more
than one slide to hide at a time.

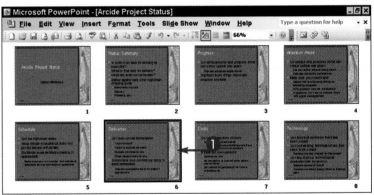

**2** Click **Slide Show**.

**3** Click **Hide Slide**.

A line appears through the slide number,
which indicates it will not display when
you show the presentation.

To redisplay the slide, you can repeat
steps **1** to **3**.

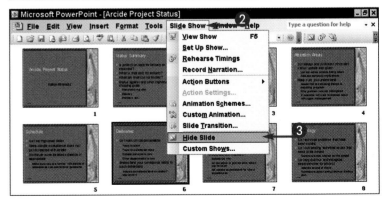

In Slide Sorter view you can view more or
less of the slides in your presentation if you
change the Zoom level. If you want to view
a great many slides, you can select a smaller
zoom percentage.

**When you are trying to find a particular
slide, for example, it is often useful to see
very small thumbnails so all or most of
the slides in the presentation appear on a
single page.**

ts in slide are close
hey appear.

## Zoom In the View

① With a PowerPoint presentation open in
Slide Sorter view, click **View**.

② Click **Zoom**.

● You can also click the Zoom field ☑ on the
Standard toolbar and select a percentage.

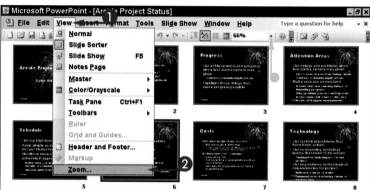

The Zoom dialog box appears.

③ Click a preset.

● You can also use the spinner arrows (⬍)
or type a percentage here.

④ Click **OK**.

The slides are displayed at the chosen
zoom level.

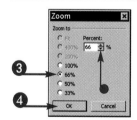

When you are working in Slide Sorter view it is sometimes useful to go to Normal view where you can view a slide in detail.

**Although you can select a slide and then use the Normal view icon, these steps shows a faster way to display an individual slide.**

## Go to an Individual Slide

① With a PowerPoint presentation open in Slide Sorter view, double-click the slide you want to display in Normal view.

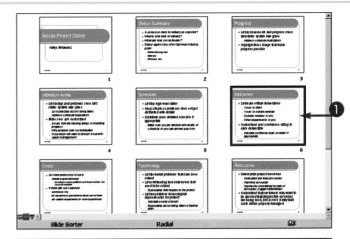

● The slide is displayed in the Normal view slide pane.

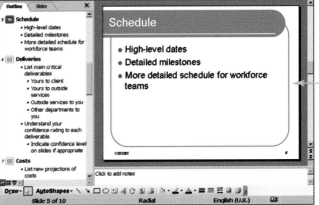

# Show/Hide Grayscale

Sometimes in a presentation with a lot of color in the background or a lot of text, it is easier to work with thumbnails in Slide Sorter view in grayscale or black and white.

**Grayscale uses black, white, and gray that indicates shading. Black and white is purely black and white so subtle shadings are left out.**

Show/Hide Grayscale

❶ With a PowerPoint presentation open in Slide Sorter view, click **View**.

❷ Click **Color/Grayscale**.

❸ Click **Grayscale** or click **Pure Black and White**.

The presentation appears in grayscale or black and white depending on your choice.

A floating toolbar also appears.

● You can also click the **Color/Grayscale** icon (▣) and select the option you prefer from the list that appears.

❹ Depending on which view you are in, click **Close Grayscale View** or **Close Black and White View** on the toolbar.

The presentation appears again in color.

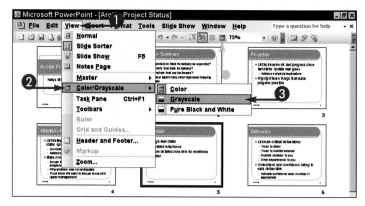

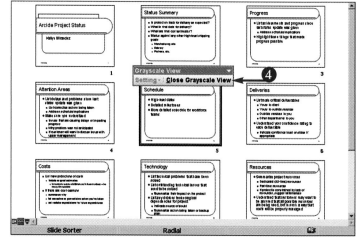

# Insert a Summary Slide

You create a summary slide with a single click in Slide Show view.

**A summary slide includes all slide titles from the presentation. It can be a useful overview for those viewing your presentation.**

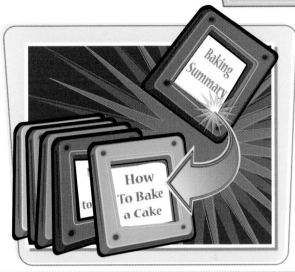

① With a PowerPoint presentation open in Slide Show view, click **Edit**.

② Click **Select All**.

All slides in the presentation are selected.

*Note: To create a summary slide in the Outline tab, see Chapter 4.*

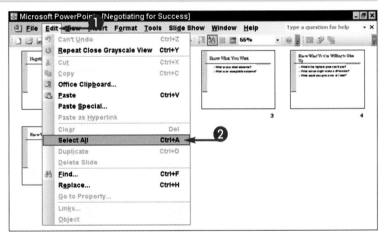

③ Click the **Summary Slide** icon ().

● A summary slide appears at the beginning of the presentation.

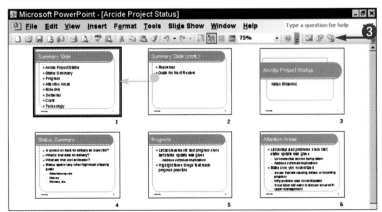

# Add Actions to Slides

Animations and transitions place action into your presentation. Instead of using static bullet points alone, animation effects manipulate text and objects on your slides, while transitions add an interesting effect every time you change from one slide to another. You can also insert movies, sounds, and hyperlinks to other programs or documents into your slides to move beyond static text.

# Understanding Animations and Action Buttons

*Animation* in PowerPoint terms is not like an animated cartoon or feature film. This animation is simply a way of moving text or objects around on your slides.

## What Is Animation?

You might animate a set of bullet points, for example, to slide in from the top of the screen, displaying one bullet point at a time. You can also animate a piece of clip art to move across your screen from left to right, or use an animation to cause a slide title or your company logo to spin around on the slide.

## When to Use Animation in a Presentation

Animations help you add emphasis to text or an object on your slide. They also help get your audience's attention back if it drifts after a long explanation or technical discussion. You should avoid overusing animations, which makes your presentation seem busy and can distract viewers from the presentation's content. Use animations sparingly and they will serve as attention grabbers that help the pace of your overall presentation.

## Using Animation Schemes

PowerPoint contains some built-in animation *schemes* that you can apply to all the text placeholders on a slide, or to all slides. You cannot, however, apply them to individual objects. PowerPoint offers three categories of animation schemes: Subtle, Moderate, and Exciting. The subtle schemes include effects such as fading in, or appearing on the slide and then dimming. Moderate effects include zooming in on a heading or having text unfold. Exciting effects have much more action. For example, an object may bounce or pinwheel onto the slide.

## Build Custom Animations

You can apply custom animations to individual objects, such as an inserted picture or table object, as well as to text placeholders. You can apply a different custom animation to each object on your slide, which is something you cannot do with an animation scheme. PowerPoint groups custom animations into four types: Entrance, Exit, Emphasis, and Motion Paths.

## Modify Animation Effects

Custom animations also provide more control over how you start playing the animation, the direction or amount of motion, and the speed of the animation. You can set an animation to play only when you click the object during a slide show, or to play with or right after the previous animation.

## How Action Buttons Work

*Action buttons* provide a different kind of action than animations. You can draw these AutoShapes on a slide and then select an action that occurs when you click the button during a slide show. For example, clicking the button might cause your presentation to jump back to the first slide or to open another presentation or Web page. You might use an action button to jump to your summary slide from the middle of your presentation to remind people of the overall agenda; or use an action button to open a support document.

## Preview Animations and Action Buttons

It is important that you preview how your animations and action buttons work during a slide show *before* you give your presentation. Choosing the right effects and making sure they run the way you expect without distracting the viewer can make the difference between a polished presentation and a sloppy one. Animation Task panes contain a Play button you can use to preview the animation effects as well as a Slide Show button to display the slide in that view. For action buttons, you have to switch to Slide Show view and click the button while running the show to verify its behavior.

## Run Animations or Action Buttons During a Slide Show

Animation schemes always play when a slide first appears in a presentation. You can set up custom animations to play when the slide appears, or with or after a previous custom animation. Finally, you can click an action button to activate it.

# Apply an Animation Scheme

Animation schemes are a quick and easy way to apply an animation effect to all objects on a slide or to all slides in your presentation. You use the Slide Design-Animation Scheme task pane to apply these schemes.

Animation schemes typically use the named effect, such as pinwheel or bounce, to the slide title, and a simpler effect to bullet points, such as having them slide up into place. This keeps the animations from distracting the viewer from the presentation's content.

## Apply an Animation Scheme

**1** Click **Format**.

**2** Click **Slide Design**.

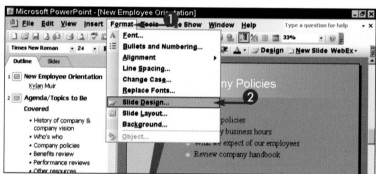

The Slide Design Task pane appears.

**3** Click the **Animation Schemes** link.

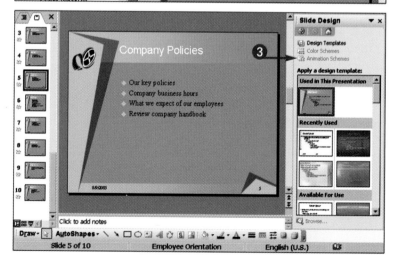

The Slide Design-Animation Schemes Task pane opens.

④ Click a scheme.

● PowerPoint previews the scheme.

⑤ Click **Apply to All Slides**.

PowerPoint applies the effect to the entire presentation.

⑥ Click **Slide Show**.

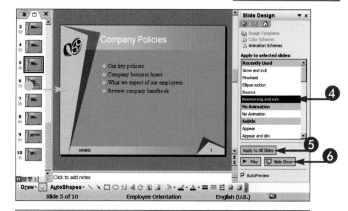

● The Slide Show view appears and the animation scheme plays.

⑦ Press Esc.

The slide show ends.

 TIPS

**I notice an option labeled AutoPreview in the Animation Schemes Task pane. What does it do?**

This is selected by default. When you first click an animation scheme, **AutoPreview** runs the animation immediately to show you what it looks like. If you turn it off by clicking the option (☑ changes to ☐), you have to click **Play** to preview the effect on that slide manually (see the next task), or run the slide show to preview it. For more on previewing the slide manually, see the next section "Preview an Animation Scheme."

**What are the benefits and drawbacks of applying an animation scheme to all slides in a presentation?**

On the plus side, using the same animation adds a consistency to your presentation, much as similar fonts or colors on every slide do. If you were to use a different animation on every slide, it becomes very busy indeed. The disadvantage is that the action begins to lose its effectiveness in a longer presentation. Consider using a different animation for each section of your presentation, or using animations only on slides that require special emphasis.

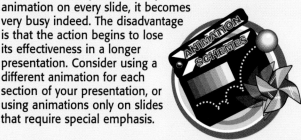

# Preview an Animation Scheme

You can play the animation in Normal view without having to start the slide show, or you can run the slide show using a button in the Animation Task pane.

**By default, a selected animation scheme goes through an AutoPreview when you first apply it. However, if you turn off AutoPreview in the Animation Schemes Task pane or you want to see the AutoPreview again, you have to know how to play it.**

Preview an Animation Scheme

① With the Slide Design-Animation Schemes Task pane displayed, click an animation scheme.

*Note: See the section "Apply an Animation Scheme" to display the Slide Design-Animation Schemes Task pane.*

● If you click **AutoPreview** (☐ changes to ☑ ), the animation previews.

② Click **Play**.

The animation previews again.

③ Click **Slide Show**.

● The slide appears in Slide Show view running the animation.

④ Press **Esc**.

The show ends.

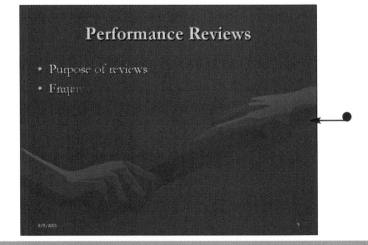

You can apply a custom animation to any selected element on a slide. A custom animation allows for more control over the animation effect.

**If you apply several custom animations to objects on a single slide, you can then set those animations up to play in any order you like.**

## Add a Custom Animation

**①** Click **Slide Show**.

**②** Click **Custom Animation**.

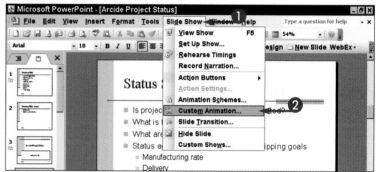

The Custom Animation task pane appears.

**③** Click an object on the slide.

You can select any kind of object: for example, a placeholder, text box, picture, or WordArt.

**④** Click **Add Effect**.

**⑤** Click a category.

**⑥** Click an effect.

PowerPoint applies the effect and previews it on the slide.

The animation appears in the Custom Animation Task pane and animation symbols appear next to the object.

Numbers in the animation symbols indicate in which order the animation will play.

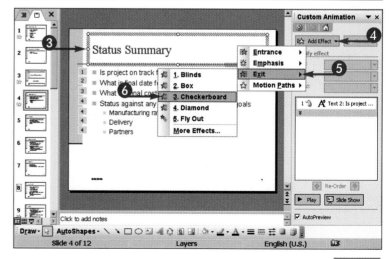

# Set Up a Custom Animation

After you apply a custom animation, you can set up several of its characteristics. You can control what initiates the animation and the speed at which the animation plays.

**You can also control the degree or style of the effect of the animation. For example, if the effect you choose increases the font size of a title, you can set the percentage of increase.**

## Set Up a Custom Animation

① With a custom animation applied to an object on a slide, click here.

*Note: To apply an animation, see the section "Add a Custom Animation."*

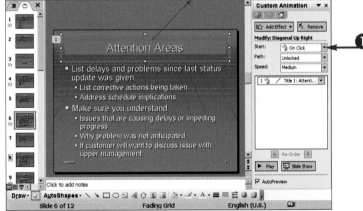

② Click an option for starting the animation when running a slide show:

You can click **On Click** to start the animation when you click your mouse.

You can click **With Previous** to start the animation at the same time as the previous animation.

You can click **After Previous** to start the animation when the previous animation finishes.

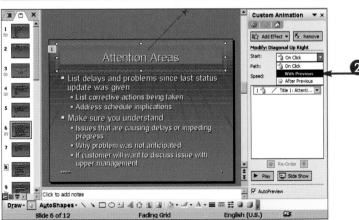

**3** Click here and select a path option.

In this example, **Locked** is selected.

This field changes the title depending on the effect you set.

PowerPoint applies the setting.

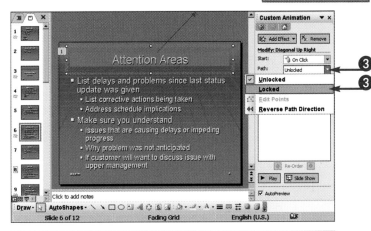

**4** Click here and select your preferred speed.

This example shows **Fast** selected.

● You can click **Play** to preview your settings.

The animation plays.

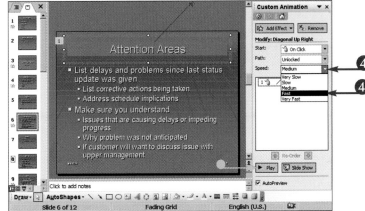

---

**TIPS**

**If I have no previous animation and choose to start this animation with or after the previous animation, what happens?**

The animation plays when the slide first appears during the slide show. However, if you make one of these choices, remember that if you later add another animation on the slide and forget you have set the second one to start with or after the previous one, they may not play in the order you want. For this reason, it is a good idea to preview the entire presentation before you show it to be sure it runs as expected.

**What if I want an animation to play 10 seconds after the previous one ends and run twice?**

Click ▼ to the right of the animation in the list and then click **Timing**. In the dialog box that appears, click the **Timing** tab and type **10** (for 10 seconds) in the Delay field. Click in the **Repeat** field and select the number of times you want the animation to repeat. When you click **OK** to close the dialog box, PowerPoint applies the delay timing.

After you have created more than one
custom animation, you can reorganize
the order in which the effects play
when the slide is displayed.

**When you reorganize the order of animation
effects, you should also verify how each
effect is started to be sure the sequence runs
as you had intended. The drop-down menu
you can access from each item in the effects
list provides commands that modify the
animation behavior.**

## Reorder Animations

**①** With the Custom Animation Task pane displayed
and several animations applied, click an animation.

*Note: See the section "Apply an Animation Scheme" to display the
Slide Design-Animation Schemes Task pane.*

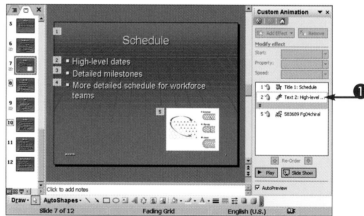

**②** Click either the **Move Up** icon (⬆) or the
**Move Down** icon (⬇).

The item moves up or down in the list accordingly.

*Note: If no animations appear below the item, ⬇ is unavailable.*

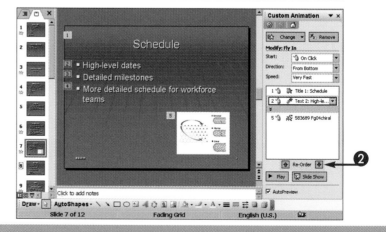

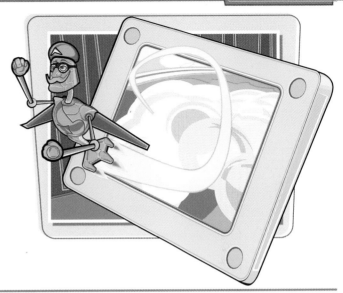

If you change your mind you can remove both custom animations and animation schemes. If you apply a custom animation and decide you want to use another animation, you have to remove the first one, or you end up with two animations on that single object.

**With animation schemes, on the other hand, you can only apply one to a slide. If you apply another scheme, the first is automatically replaced.**

## Remove an Animation

### REMOVE AN ANIMATION SCHEME

①  Display the slide from which you want to remove an animation scheme.

②  With the Slide Design-Animation Schemes Task pane displayed in the Apply to Selected Slides list, under the No Animation heading click **No Animation**.

*Note: See the section "Apply an Animation Scheme" to display the Slide Design-Animation Schemes Task pane.*

The animation scheme is removed.

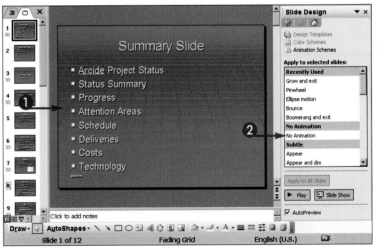

### REMOVE A CUSTOM ANIMATION

①  Click **Slide Show**.

②  Click **Custom Animation**.

The Custom Animation task pane appears.

③  Click an animation effect in the list.

④  Click **Remove**.

PowerPoint removes the animation effect from the object.

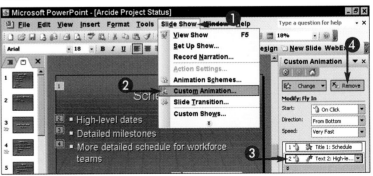

# Insert an Action Button

Action buttons are a quick and easy way to allow you to jump to a slide with related content while giving a presentation. You can also use them to open a Web page, another presentation, or another type of document.

**Remember that if you want to go to a Web page, you have to have an Internet connection available when you give the presentation. If you want to open another document, you must have it available on your hard disk or a removable storage disc. You can also run another program, but again, you must have it installed on the computer you use to show the presentation.**

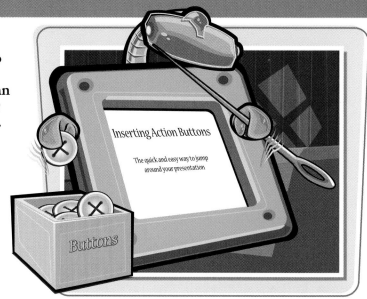

## Insert an Action Button

### INSERT A BUTTON

**①** Click **AutoShapes**.

**②** Click **Action Buttons**.

The Action Button palette appears.

**③** Click a button style.

**④** Click the slide and drag it to draw the button.

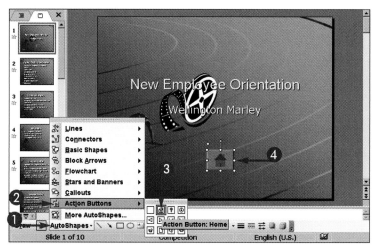

### ESTABLISH A HYPERLINK

An action button is drawn and the Action Settings dialog box appears.

**⑤** Click **Hyperlink to** (⬡ changes to ⦿).

**⑥** Click here and select what should appear when the action button is clicked.

Depending on your choice, two things can happen; for example, if you click **Last Slide**, that setting then appears in the field. If you click **URL**, a dialog box appears for you to type a URL.

**RUN A PROGRAM**

1 Perform steps **1** to **4** on the previous page.

The Action Settings dialog box appears.

2 Click **Run Program** (○ changes to ◉).

3 Click **Browse**.

The Select a Program to Run dialog box appears.

4 Click here to locate a program.

5 Click a program name.

6 Click **OK**.

You return to the Action Settings dialog box.

7 Click **OK** in the Action Settings dialog box.

● The action button appears on the slide.

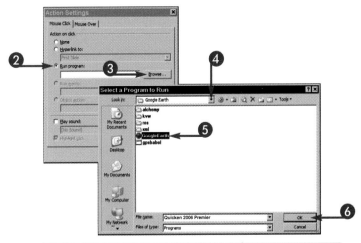

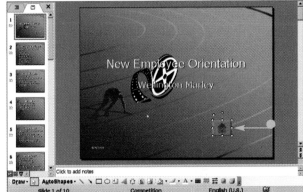

 **TIPS**

**I want to include a hyperlink, but I do not want to clutter the slide with an action button icon. How can I do that?**

You can insert a text hyperlink on your slide. Using this feature, you can, for example, make your slide title function as a hyperlink, clicking it instead of an action button during a slide show and following the link instead of an action button. See the section "Insert a Hyperlink" for more about this.

**Is there a quicker way to access the Action Button palette?**

Yes. You can actually make the Action Button palette a floating toolbar. When you do, it is onscreen until you close it. With the Action Button palette displayed, click the dotted line ( ▫▫▫▫▫▫▫▫▫▫ ) across the top of it and drag it away from the AutoShapes menu. To get rid of it, click the **Close** icon (✕) in the corner.

# Understanding Transitions

Transitions offer a way to add variety to your presentation. With transitions, you can modify how slides are displayed when they first appear. You can also set up PowerPoint to play sounds when a transition occurs, or to time a transition to occur at various speeds.

## What Is a Transition?

A transition is an effect that occurs when you move from one slide to another. You have experienced transitions in movies, when you see the screen dissolve from one image to another, or you see an image seem to wipe across the screen to reveal another scene.

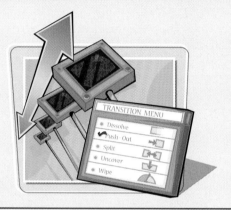

## Different Ways to Advance Slides

Transitions are also used to control when slides advance. You can choose to have a slide advance on a mouse click, or to advance with preset timing. If you plan to show a presentation at a kiosk, for example, you might have slides advance every 30 seconds.

## Control Speed

You can control how fast a transition occurs. Effects such as a fade-in will be very different if you have a slow fade-in or a fast fade-in. One gives viewers more of a separation from the previous topic, another keeps the presentation moving right along.

## Add Sounds

Adding a sound when a transition occurs can give emphasis, help you make a point, or provide an element of surprise. For example, display the slide that tells your viewers you have broken last year's sales record while playing a drum roll.

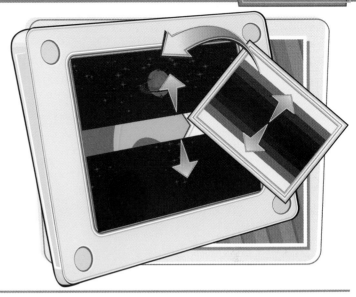

To add a transition, you must first display the slide that you want to appear with the selected transition. You can also select several slides and then apply a transition effect to all of them. Finally, you have the option of applying a transition to all slides in the presentation.

**There is an option of applying a Random Transition. If you select this and apply it to all slides, for example, PowerPoint randomly applies a different transition effect throughout the presentation.**

### Add a Transition

**①** Click **Slide Show**.

**②** Click **Slide Transition**.

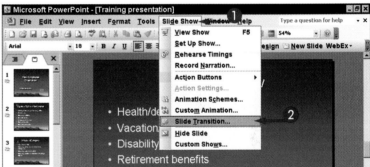

The Slide Transition Task pane appears.

**③** Click a transition in the list.

● PowerPoint applies the transition to the slide or selected slides, and the effect previews.

● To apply the transition to all slides, click **Apply to All Slides**.

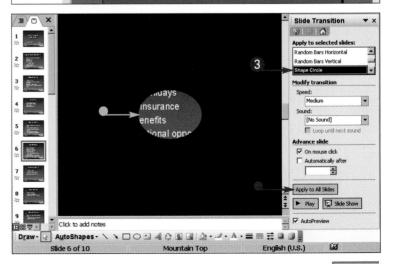

# Remove a Transition

Sometimes while designing a presentation, you apply a transition and then decide that it just does not work. PowerPoint lets you easily remove any transition in your presentation if you change your mind.

1 Click **Slide Show**.

2 Click **Slide Transition**.

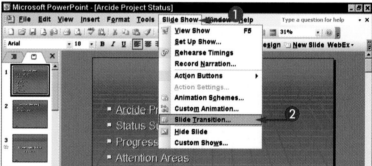

The Slide Transition Task pane appears.

3 Click **No Transition**.

PowerPoint removes any existing transition.

● To remove all transitions from the entire presentation, you can click **Apply to All Slides**.

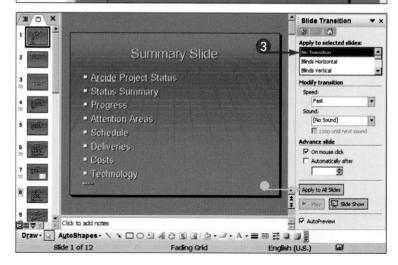

When you are running a presentation, you can use two methods to advance from slide to slide. Both are set up in the Slide Transition Task pane.

**You can manually advance slides by clicking your mouse or the onscreen navigation arrows that appear in Slide Show view. Or you can set up timing that advances your slides automatically after a certain number of seconds has passed.**

## Advance a Slide After a Set Time Interval

**1** Select a slide.

**2** With the Slide Transition Task pane displayed, click **Automatically after** (☐ changes to ☑ ).

*Note: See the section "Remove a Transition" to display the Slide Transition Task pane.*

**3** Click the spinner arrows (🔂) to set the time interval.

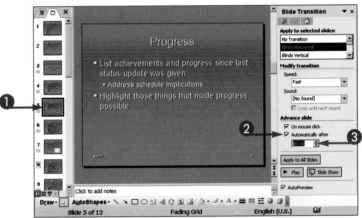

**4** Click **Slide Sorter** view (▦).

● A notation of the set time interval now appears under the slide, along with a star indicating an animation is applied.

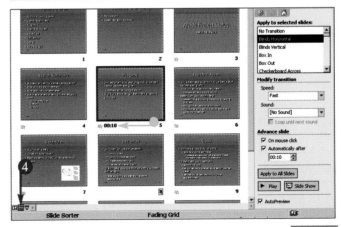

# Insert Movie and Sound Clips

To make your presentation more lively, you can insert movie or sound clips into your PowerPoint file and then play them during a presentation. These are part of the Clip Art feature.

**You can also use the Media Clip icon in any content placeholder to insert movie and sound clips. See Chapter 5 for more about using placeholders.**

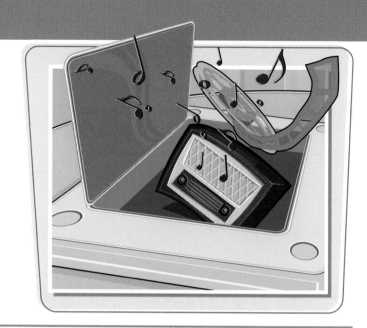

## Insert Movie and Sound Clips

### INSERT A MOVIE OR SOUND CLIP

1. Display the slide on which you want to insert a clip in Normal view.

2. Click **Insert**.

3. Click **Movies and Sounds**.

4. Click either **Movie from Clip Organizer** or **Sound from Clip Organizer**.

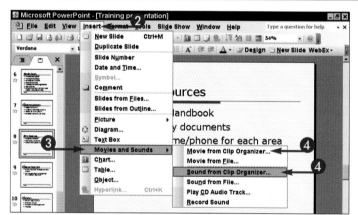

The Clip Art Task pane appears.

5. Click the clip you want.

● You can click and drag to scroll down the list of files.

**Note:** If you are inserting a sound file, a message appears asking how you want the sound to be started during the show. Click either **Automatically** or **When Clicked** and then click **OK**.

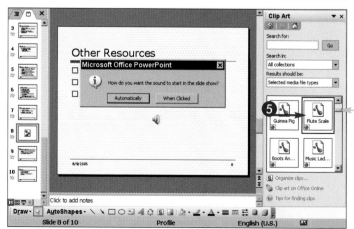

## PLAY A MOVIE OR SOUND CLIP

● If you want to find clips on a particular subject, you can type that word in the Search for box and click **Go**.

● PowerPoint inserts the clip on the slide.

**6** Click **Slide Show** (🖳).

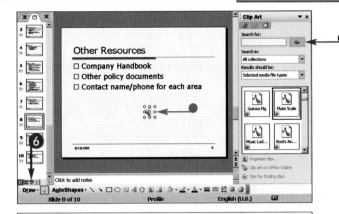

The view changes to Slide Show. If you insert a movie, it plays repeatedly.

**7** Click any sound icon (🔊).

The sound plays.

*Note: If you selected **Automatically** for a sound clip on the previous page, the sound plays without you clicking it.*

**8** Press Esc .

The slide show ends.

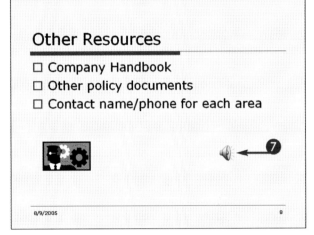

**Other Resources**

☐ Company Handbook
☐ Other policy documents
☐ Contact name/phone for each area

8/9/2005

**I have a sound file I got off the Internet. Can I insert it?**

Yes. You can click **Insert**, **Movies and Sounds**, and on the submenu that appears click **Sound from File**. Then locate the folder to which you downloaded the file, click the file, and then click **OK**. You see a dialog box that asks if you want the file started automatically or when you click it. Make your selection and the file inserts on your slide.

**What if I want to get both movies and sounds related to sports? Do I have to do two different searches?**

No. You can specify that both movies and sounds should be searched. In the Clip Art Task pane, click the arrow in the Results Should Be field and make sure that you select both movies and sounds in the list that appears. You can also specify that clip art and photographs be searched or not, as you prefer.

# Insert a Hyperlink

A *hyperlink*, also called simply a link, is actually a piece of Hypertext Markup Language (HTML) that displays another document when you click it.

**In PowerPoint, clicking a hyperlink displays another slide in the current presentation, opens another presentation or document saved in another format, opens a blank e-mail form, or opens a Web page.**

① Click to select a title or text placeholder on a slide.

② Click **Insert**.

③ Click **Hyperlink**.

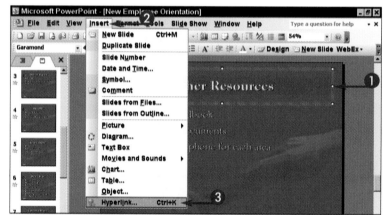

The Insert Hyperlink dialog box appears.

④ Click an item in the **Link to** list to specify the kind of link to insert.

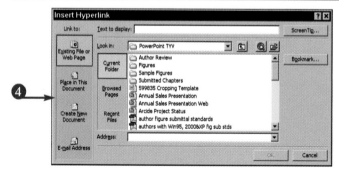

Depending on what you select, different options appear.

⑤ Locate or type the slide, document, Web page, or e-mail address in the appropriate fields.

⑥ Click **OK**.

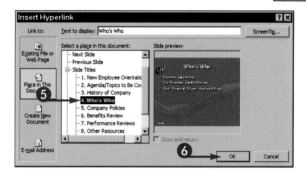

● PowerPoint places the link on your slide.

**Note:** When you enter Slide Show view, you can click the text to follow the link.

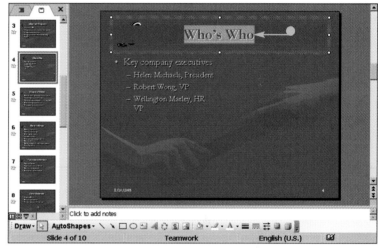

**TIPS**

**How do I remove a link to a file on a slide but leave the link text?**

With the hyperlink placeholder selected, press **Ctrl** + **K** to open the Insert Hyperlink dialog box. Click **Remove Link**, and then click **OK**. The link text remains, but the link itself has been removed.

**I do not want to enter a lot of text for the link itself, but I would like to let the person running the presentation know exactly what it leads to. How can I do that?**

Create a screen tip. In the Insert Hyperlink dialog box, click the **Screen Tip** button and enter as much text as you like in the dialog box that appears. Click **OK** and proceed to save the link. Now when the person running the show holds the mouse over the link, the tip appears in a little box. This is a convenient way to let them know what will happen if they click the link.

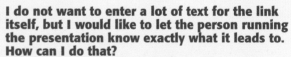

# Set Up and Run a Slide Show

After you add all your slide content, tweak your slide design, and add graphics, animations, and transitions, you are almost done. In this chapter you take the final steps to set up your presentation options and, finally, run your slide show!

# Select a Show Type and Show Options

Before you run your show for the first time, you should check the settings for the type of show, and some of the options for running the show. These options include whether the show should repeat continuously, whether you want to use narration and animations, and the annotation pen color.

**The pen is a tool you use when you run a slide show, allowing you to draw or write on the slides to call attention to a point or write in more information.**

## Select a Show Type and Show Options

1 Click **Slide Show**.

2 Click **Set Up Show**.

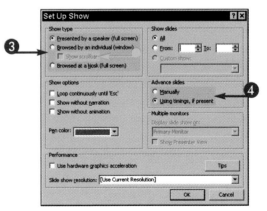

The Set Up Show dialog box appears.

3 Select whether you want to have a presenter run the show, a viewer browse the show on a computer, or a viewer view the show at a kiosk (⊙ changes to ⊙).

● If you choose to let viewers browse the show, you can click the **Show Scrollbar** option (☐ changes to ☑) with the computer option.

4 Select whether you want to manually move through the slides with navigation buttons or a mouse, or advance slides based on timing (⊙ changes to ⊙).

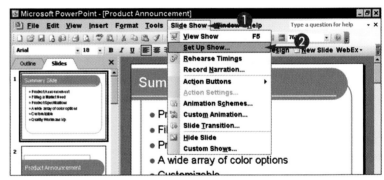

**5** Select whether you want to loop through the show continuously, show it without narration, or show it without animation (☐ changes to ☑).

**6** Click here and select a pen color from the palette.

***Note:*** *This item is not available if you select any show type other than Presented by a Speaker.*

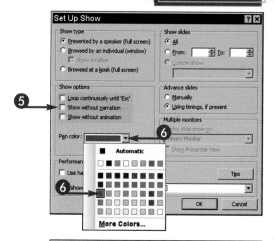

**7** Click **OK**.

Your show is set up.

## Why would I want to show my presentation without animation?

Animations are fun, but on slower computer systems, they may run slowly and delay your show. If you are using an older computer to present your show, preview it to be sure that animations run smoothly. If they do not, change this setting to avoid any problems.

## What is a loop and why would I use it?

Looping is a term for running media — a song, video, or slide show — over and over again from beginning to end. If you plan to show your presentation at an informational booth or kiosk where passersby may stop, watch a bit, and then move on, you want the presentation to keep going until you stop it. To do this, select the **Loop continuously until 'Esc'** option (☐ changes to ☑) under Show Options.

# Specify Slide Show Content

Sometimes you create a larger presentation, but decide that for a particular audience or in a particular setting you only want to show some of the slides. You can specify ranges of slides to run, or you can set up and save custom shows and easily choose the one you need from a list of custom shows.

**After you create a show, you must tell PowerPoint to run it. See the next steps for that setting.**

## Specify Slide Show Content

**CREATE A CUSTOM SHOW**

1 Click **Slide Show**.

2 Click **Custom Shows**.

The Custom Shows dialog box appears.

3 Click **New**.

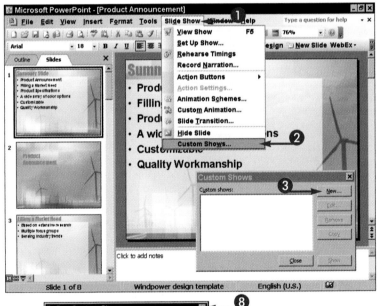

4 In the Define Custom Show dialog box, type a custom show name.

5 Click a slide.

6 Click **Add**.

You can repeat step **5** to add all the slides you want to show.

● You can click a slide you have added and then click the **Move Up** (⬆) and **Move Down** (⬇) icons to change the slide show order.

7 Click **OK**.

8 Click the **Close** icon (✖) in the Custom Shows dialog box to save the show.

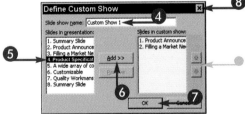

## SPECIFY WHICH SLIDES TO SHOW

① Click **Slide Show**.

② Click **Set Up Show**.

The Set Up Show dialog box appears.

③ Select whether to show all slides or a range of slides, or a custom show (○ changes to ●).

● You can click the spinner arrows (🖫) to set the first and last slide numbers.

④ Click **OK**.

Your settings are saved.

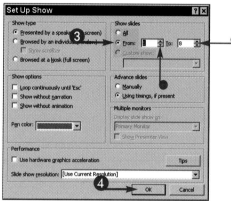

---

**TIPS**

**Some slides display very slowly. Why is that?**

Slides that use animations that involve scaling, fading, or rotating actions take more memory and can cause you problems. In addition, using gradient fills in objects instead of solid color fills may slow down the display of your slides. Select other options for these to speed things up.

**What if I do not want to show a slide right in the middle of my presentation? I cannot specify a range that excludes that one slide. Do I have to create a custom show adding every slide to it but that one?**

No. With a large presentation it takes quite a while to build a custom show that excludes only one slide. In this case, just hide the slide. Click the **Slide Show View** (🖳) or the **Normal View** (🖾) and select the slide. Click **Slide Show**, and then click **Hide Slide**. The slide does not display when you run the show.

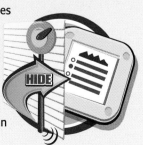

You may want to use two monitors for your presentation, one you run the show from and one the audience sees. This allows you to run another program while the show runs if you want, and to use Presenter view with tools to make running a show easier. You can also set your screen resolution to show more or less fine detail.

**Note that you have to set up PowerPoint to support multiple monitors, as shown in these steps, before making these settings.**

### Work with Multiple Monitors and Resolution

**SET UP MULTIPLE MONITORS**

① Click **Slide Show**.

② Click **Set Up Show**.

The Set Up Show dialog box displays.

③ Click here and select the monitor to show the presentation on.

④ Click the **Show Presenter View** option (☐ changes to ☑) to display Presenter view.

⑤ Click **OK**.

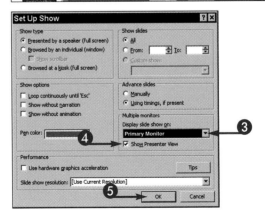

## SET RESOLUTION

1 Follow steps **1** and **2** on the previous page to display the Set Up Show dialog box.

2 Click here and select a resolution from the list.

3 Click **OK**.

PowerPoint saves your settings.

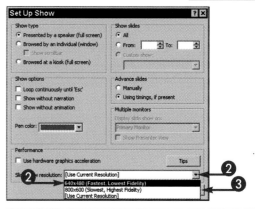

When you run your slide show the resolution is as you set it up.

# Summary Slide

- **Product Announcement**
- **Filling a Market Need**
- **Product Specifications**
- **A wide array of color options**
- **Customizable**
- **Quality Workmanship**

 **TIPS**

**I notice a checkbox for hardware graphics acceleration in the Set Up Show dialog box. What is it used for?**

If your computer has a video adapter with a graphics coprocessor, it can help speed up display on your monitor. If you have such hardware in your computer, click the **Use Hardware Graphics Acceleration** option ( ☐ changes to ☑ ) to take advantage of it. Look in your owner's manual or check the list of hardware drivers in Windows Control Panel to see if an accelerator is available to you.

**I placed a diagram in my speaker's notes but it is not there in Presenter view when I use multiple monitors. Why not?**

Only text notes display in Presenter view. You can display the notes page by clicking **View** and then **Notes Pages** while in Normal view. Next, switch between the **Slide Show View** (🖵) and **Normal View** (🖵) icons on your monitor, if you want.

# Record a Narration

If you will not be presenting your PowerPoint show in person, or you are presenting it on the Web, you may want to record a narration that talks the viewer through your key points. Recording a narration is easy to do, and also sets up your presentation to advance automatically to the next slide at the end of the current slide's narration.

**After it is recorded, remember to set the narration options in the Set Up Show dialog box to ensure that the Show Without Narration option is *not* selected.**

## Record a Narration

① Plug a microphone into your computer.

② Click **Slide Show**.

③ Click **Record Narration**.

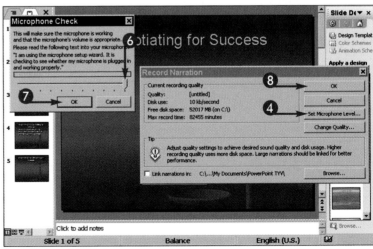

The Record Narration dialog box appears.

④ Click **Set Microphone Level**.

The Microphone Check dialog box opens.

⑤ Read the suggested text into your microphone.

PowerPoint checks that your microphone is working properly.

⑥ Click and drag the slider (⬜) to change microphone volume.

⑦ Click **OK**.

⑧ Click **OK** in the Record Narration dialog box.

A message appears asking if you want the show to begin to run with the currently displayed/selected slide.

**9** Click either **Current Slide** or **First Slide**.

**10** Speak your narration into your microphone, moving slides forward when you get to a new topic.

**11** When you finish the presentation, press `Esc`.

A message appears asking if you want to save the timings.

**12** Click **Save**.

**13** Click the **Slide Sorter View** icon (▦).

Slide Sorter view appears.

● Timings are shown beneath each slide reflecting the length of recorded narration for each.

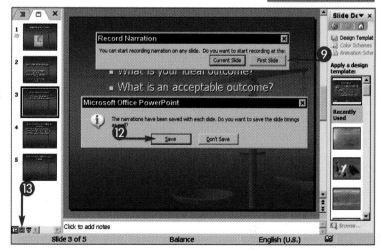

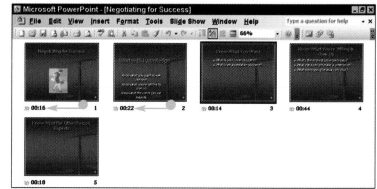

**TIPS**

**My narration quality is a little poor. Is there anything I can do about this?**

You can set the quality level for your narration. However, keep in mind that higher quality recordings mean bigger presentation files. To adjust quality, click **Change Quality** in the Record Narration dialog box. Higher Khz settings provide higher quality.

**My presentation file got way too big with a lot of sound files and animations in it. What should I do?**

One obvious option is to lose some of these effects. But if they are all absolutely necessary, you can add links to audio files on your slides instead of using the Record Narration feature. That way you are linking to files stored on your hard drive, not within the presentation itself. Just be sure to copy both the presentation and any linked files when you save the presentation to CD, or use your computer to run the presentation; otherwise the sound becomes unavailable to you.

# Run a Slide Show

You have typed a lot of text, inserted graphics and animations, and made various settings. By doing all this, you have built a slide show that is only a click away. But how, exactly, does it all come together?

## Display Your Presentation

To input your material into PowerPoint and display your slide show, all you have to do is click the Slide Show icon (🖳). Then, whatever slide you have currently displayed in Normal view or selected in Slide Sorter view, displays full screen in Slide Show view. All the toolbars and menus and panes go away, and you are left with only your slide contents — which was the whole point of all this work, after all!

## Navigate the Presentation

Essentially, presenting a slide show involves moving from one slide to another. You can do this either in sequence, or by jumping to slides using action buttons or the Navigation menu in Slide Show view. You can control how you move through the show manually by using timings you have saved with each slide, or through the options you select in Slide Show Setup, discussed in this chapter. For more on using action buttons, see Chapter 10. For more on the Slide Show view, see Chapter 14.

## Interact with the Presentation

During a presentation you can pause it, stop it, hide it, display a different program, or add annotations. The annotation feature uses a technology called ink, which allows you to draw arrows, words, or just about anything on your screen and save those annotations with the presentation. This is useful if, for example, you want to add some bright ideas that come up during the presentation to your own and keep a record of them. You can also add speaker's notes from within the presentation if you prefer to type rather than draw your comments. See Chapter 14 for more about running a show.

## End the Show

You can end the show at any time and save any speaker's notes or ink annotations you have made for future reference. Now all you have to do is sit back and accept the congratulations coming your way for a great presentation.

You can save a presentation to a CD or to your hard drive in a format that can include both files you have linked your presentation to, and a PowerPoint viewer. This viewer allows you to show the presentation even on a computer that does not have PowerPoint.

**You can also download the PowerPoint viewer from Microsoft's Web site at www.microsoft.com.**

## Package a Presentation

**①** Click **File**.

**②** Click **Package for CD**.

The Package for CD dialog box appears.

**③** Type the presentation name.

**④** Click **Add Files**.

The Add Files dialog box appears.

**⑤** Click to locate a file.

**⑥** Click a file.

*Note: All linked files and the PowerPoint viewer are included by default. Only use this feature for file formats other than PoewrPoint you may want to reference or open during the presentation.*

**⑦** Click **Add**.

**⑧** In the Package for CD dialog box, click **Copy to Folder** or **Copy to CD**.

PowerPoint saves the presentation.

If you copy to a folder, you see a dialog box that allows you to select the folder in which you want to store the file.

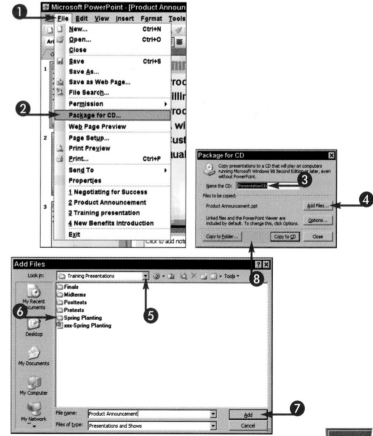

# Print Presentations

There are several reasons you might print a presentation. You may want a hard copy of your slides to review away from your computer, for example, on a plane. Or you might want to print handouts for your audience to follow during your live presentation. Finally, you might print just your presentation outline to preserve a hard copy of the presentation text.

# Using Print Preview

It is a good idea to make sure your slides and the print output you select are as you want them before you print. This is especially true of slides with colorful or dark backgrounds; printing them can use up a lot of printer ink! To see what your printout will look like before printing, use the Print Preview feature.

**1** Click **File**.

**2** Click **Print Preview**.

The Print Preview dialog box appears.

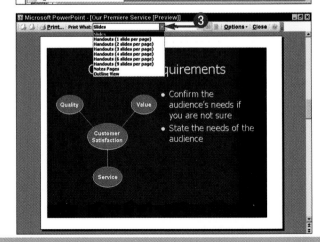

**3** Click here to select the format for printed output.

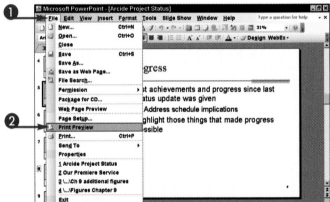

④ Click the **Next Page** icon (📄) to go to the next page of the presentation.

⑤ Click here to select the preview zoom percentage.

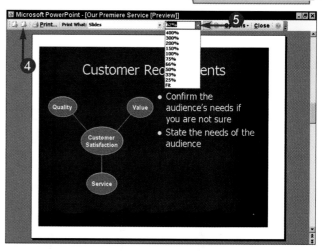

● The slide is displayed at the selected percentage.

⑥ Click here to **Print**.

The presentation is sent to your default printer in the selected output format and the Print Preview closes.

● If you are not ready to print, you can click **Close** to close the Print Preview.

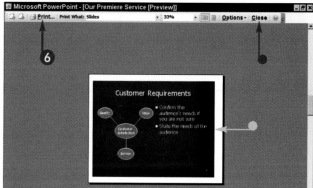

### When I use Print Preview, my cursor becomes a little magnifying glass. Why?

Slides display one at a time in Print Preview. The magnifying tool is a shortcut to zoom in and out of the slide. Click the slide when the magnifier has a plus sign and it expands to either full view or the percentage you have chosen in the Print Preview toolbar, if it is more than 100%. Click when it has a minus sign and it returns to the smaller of these two settings.

### How can I tell quickly how many pages will print if I choose to print, say, 4 handouts per page?

Look at the bottom of the Print Preview screen. It shows how many total pages will print, and which page you currently have displayed in Print Preview. So, for example, if you have 11 slides and want to print 4 to a page, it might say Print: Page 2 of 3, with 3 being the total number of pages.

# Change Page Setup and Orientation

When you print from PowerPoint you can adjust settings to size slides so you can print them on different sizes of paper. You can also change settings for the orientation. Portrait prints vertically like a business letter. Landscape prints horizontally. You can make two separate orientation settings, one for slides and one for all other formats, such as notes, handouts, and outlines.

Change Page Setup and Orientation

**SET PAPER SIZE**

① Click **File**.

② Click **Page Setup**.

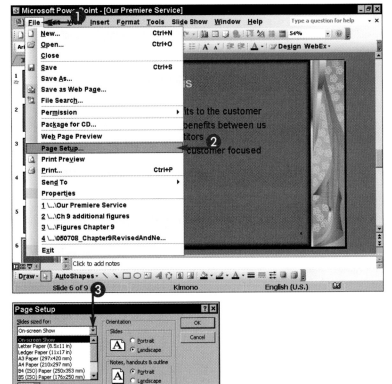

The Page Setup dialog box appears.

③ Click here and select the output size.

④ Click here to set a custom width for the print area.

⑤ Click here to select a custom height for the print area.

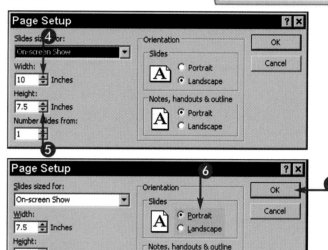

### CHANGE ORIENTATION

⑥ Click here ( ⊙ changes to ⊙ ) to change Slide orientation to Portrait.

⑦ Click ( ⊙ changes to ⊙ ) to change Notes, Handouts, and Outline orientation to Landscape.

**Note:** *Steps 6 and 7 both assume you are changing default orientation settings.*

⑧ Click **OK**.

The dialog box closes and your settings are saved.

**I changed to print in landscape, but now my titles are off center. Why?**

When you change the paper size or orientation for your slides after you have created them, it may cause objects on the slides to be positioned differently than you want them to. It is best to make size and orientation settings before you build the presentation, but if that is not possible, you should check your master slide settings. You may have to manually rearrange the objects on the master slide to make things look right again.

**If I want to make my own setting, do I have to first select something in the Slides sized for list?**

Not really. You click **Custom** in that list and then type custom measurements, but if there is some other setting in that list and you change the measurements, PowerPoint changes the Slides sized for setting to Custom for you.

You can print a single slide, your entire presentation, selected slides, or a custom show — subsets of your presentation saved within it. Slides print one per page.

**If you have a color printer available, you can print slides in color. Use the Properties button in the Print dialog box to change your designated printer.**

## Print Slides

① Click **File**.

② Click **Print**.

The Print dialog box appears.

③ Click here and select **Slides**.

④ Change any of the following settings:

● You can click here to change the number of copies to print.

● You can click any of these options (○ changes to ⊙) to print all slides, to print the currently displayed slide, to print slides you selected before opening the Print dialog box, or to print only certain slides.

● If you select only certain slides, you can type slide numbers separated by commas.

⑤ Click **OK**.

The slides print to your default printer.

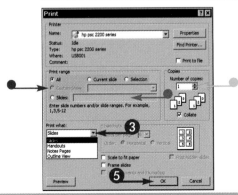

# Frame Slides

You can print slides with a frame, which places a neat borderline around the edge of the slides and defines them on a printed page.

**When you print slides by default, they print without any kind of border around them. Sometimes it is helpful to envision the defined "edge" of the slides to appreciate the balance of the elements on the design.**

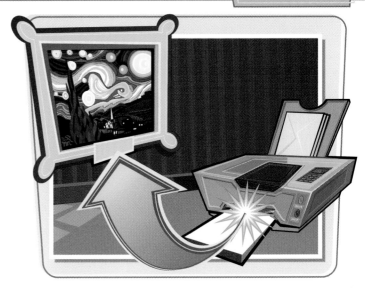

## Frame Slides

**①** Click **File**.

**②** Click **Print**.

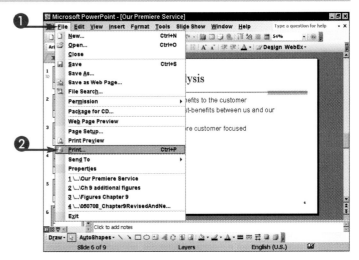

The Print dialog box opens.

**③** Click the **Frame slides** option (☐ changes to ☑) to frame slides.

**④** Click **OK**.

The slides print with frames.

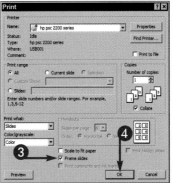

# Print
# Handouts

It is often helpful to give your audience members handouts of your presentation so they can follow along, or so they can have them for future reference. You can print from one to nine slides on a handout page.

**Printing several slides per page can save paper when you want to print numerous handouts.**

## Print Handouts

① Click **File**.

② Click **Print**.

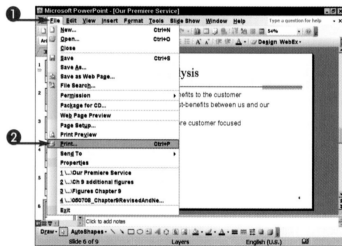

The Print dialog box appears.

③ Click here and select Handouts as the format to print.

④ Click here and select the number of slides to print per page.

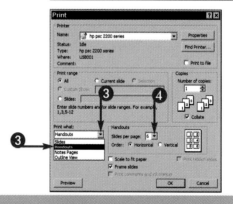

...

● The preview changes to reflect the number of slides you selected.

⑤ Click here (◯ changes to ◉) to change the order of slides from horizontal to vertical.

The preview changes to show that slides will print in order down the left side, and then continue in order down the right.

**Note:** *This option is only available to you if you select four or more slides per handout in step* **4.**

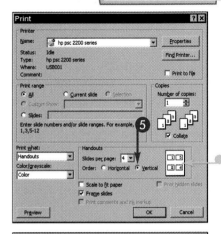

⑥ Click **OK**.

The handouts print.

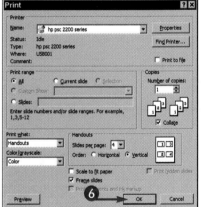

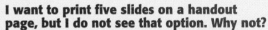

**TIPS**

**Is there any way to rearrange the appearance of multiple handouts on a page? I want to move them closer together.**

You can use the Handout Master. In Master view you can reposition the placeholders for the various handouts. See Chapter 7 for more about working with masters.

**I want to print five slides on a handout page, but I do not see that option. Why not?**

For whatever reason, Microsoft has made it possible to print 1, 2, 3, 4, 6, or 9 slides on a page, but not 5, 7, or 8. One option for you is to click **File**, and then **Send To** to send your slides to Word and move the slides around pages to get the arrangement you want.

# Print in Black and White or Grayscale

You can print a presentation in color, black and white, or grayscale. Grayscale provides some shading to help you see graphic and background elements. Black and white shows no such shading and will show no background color or pattern.

**If you are printing multiple copies of a draft presentation for review, you can avoid printing in color or using printer ink on backgrounds that do not impact the presentation contents.**

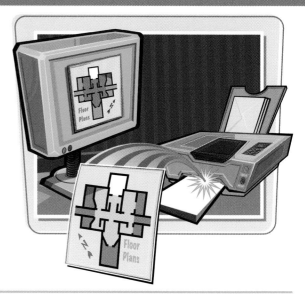

① Click **File**.

② Click **Print**.

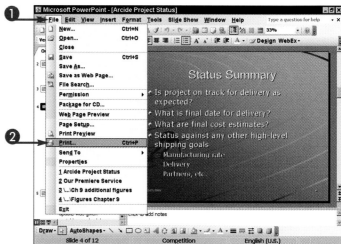

The Print dialog box appears.

③ Click here and select either **Grayscale** or **Pure Black and White**.

④ Click **OK**.

The presentation prints with your color selection.

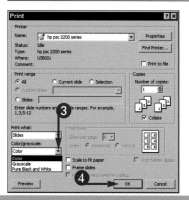

You may decide to give a presentation, but not to show every slide. For example if you have a long presentation about benefits that includes manager information, but you are showing it to hourly workers, you can hide the manager slides.

**By default, hidden slides are printed. You can easily adjust your printer settings to not print hidden slides when printing a presentation.**

**Print Hidden Slides**

1 Click **File**.

2 Click **Print**.

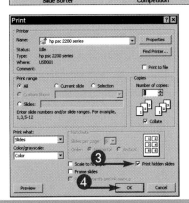

The Print dialog box appears.

3 Click **Print Hidden Slides** (☑ changes to ☐).

4 Click **OK**.

The presentation prints without hidden slides.

*Note: If there are no hidden slides in your presentation, this option is not available.*

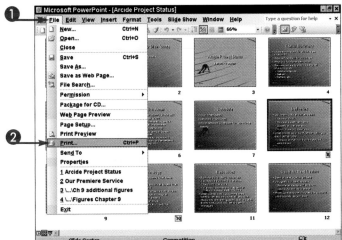

# Print
# Outline View

Sometimes you just want to focus on the presentation text and not the graphic details. Printing the Outline view is a good option in this case.

**The outline includes titles, subtitles, and bullet points, but does not include any text entered in text boxes or footers.**

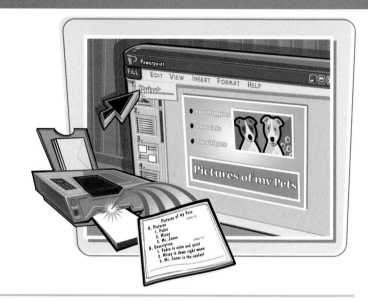

Print Outline View

**1** Click **File**.

**2** Click **Print**.

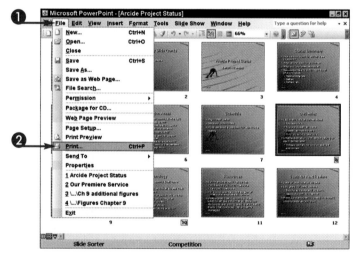

The Print dialog box appears.

**3** Click here and select **Outline View**.

**4** Click **OK**.

The Outline view prints.

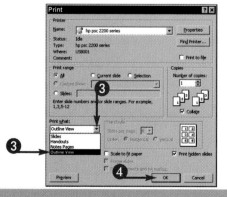

# Print Notes

The presenter of a slide show often needs a cheat sheet. You can print Notes Pages, which print one page for each slide and any notes for that slide beneath it.

**Printing a presentation with speaker's notes is a great tool for a presenter. You can reference them during the presentation, or use them to prepare before the presentation.**

## Print Notes

1 Click **File**.

2 Click **Print**.

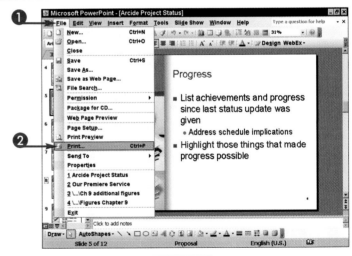

The Print dialog box appears.

3 Click here and select **Notes Pages**.

4 Click **OK**.

The slides and notes are printed.

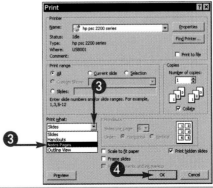

# CHAPTER 13

# Give Presentations Online

You can give PowerPoint presentations online, which allows you to reach hundreds or even thousands of people with your message. You can publish a presentation on a Web site and people can then go to that site and navigate through it. Even those who do not have access to PowerPoint can view your presentation after it is published online.

# Work with Web Presentations

With PowerPoint you can publish a presentation to the Web with no need for a Web publishing program. You can easily preview your presentation as a Web page to see how it will look in a Web browser before you publish it.

## Publish a Presentation to the Web

When you publish a presentation to the Web, you essentially save it in a Web format and post it to a Web server. People can access it at any time from around the world. You can also insert links to the presentation in other presentations or documents.

## Use the Broadcast Feature

Another way to deliver a presentation online is to use a broadcast feature that allows you to offer a live show, but this feature is only available if your computer is networked, for example, at your workplace.

## Navigate a Web Presentation

A presentation viewed in a browser automatically offers certain navigation features to those viewing it. By default, a presentation includes a list of links along the left side that you can click to go to any slide in the presentation. You can expand this list to show the entire presentation outline. You can also use navigation arrows at the bottom of the browser screen to go forward or backward in the presentation, slide by slide. Finally, you can display the presentation in Full Screen Slide Show mode.

## Make Good Use of Web Presentations

Once you publish a presentation to the Web, you can extend its impact. That is because you can then link to it from other Web pages. People visiting those pages can jump over to your presentation via the link. Talk to your Webmaster for ideas about how to link to your online presentation.

## Accommodate Browsers

Different browsers may display your presentation in slightly different ways. Depending on the fonts available, for example, the browser application may have to substitute a font you use in your presentation with one it has access to. You can set up browser support in PowerPoint when publishing a presentation, accommodating what you think will be the most commonly used browser combination.

## Change the Appearance of Your Web Presentation

You can make changes to your presentation by changing default font and color settings in PowerPoint. The color settings change the background for the Outline and Slide panes in your presentation, which by default use a black background and white fonts. You can also specify a title for your presentation that displays at the top of the Web page.

A quick way to see what your presentation will look like when viewed as a Web page is to preview it as a Web page. This helps you catch any problems with the way it displays in a browser before you publish it online.

**You can also see how your presentation colors work with the default Web presentation colors without having to first publish the presentation.**

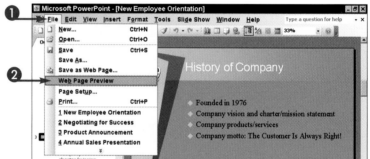

## Preview as a Web Page

**1** Click **File**.

**2** Click **Web Page Preview**.

The presentation displays in a browser window.

**3** Click the **Close** (⊠) icon.

The preview closes.

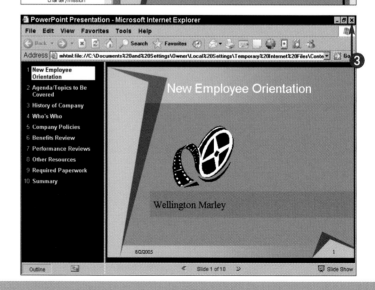

You can save your presentation in Web page format. You may do this with the idea of sending the file to people who simply double-click it to view it in a browser.

By default, when you save as a Web page, PowerPoint saves the file in the Single File Web Page format. This saves all the elements of the presentation, including text and graphics, in one file. This MHTML — Meta HTML — format is useful for e-mailing Web page files because it compresses the file to a manageable size. The option is to save as a Web page, which creates all the associated image and HTML files required for a Web page, rather than a single file.

## Save a Presentation as a Web Page

① Click **File**.

② Click **Save as Web Page**.

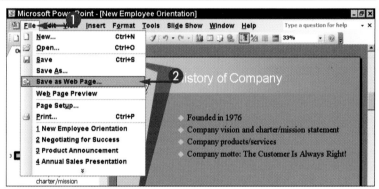

The Save As dialog box appears.

● You can click here to locate the folder to save the file to.

③ Type a filename.

④ Click **Save**.

The file is saved in Web page format.

**Note:** *The Save as type field still offers a variety of formats when you save as Web page, including regular PowerPoint presentation format; The two formats that you should use for Web pages are Single File Web Page and Web Page.*

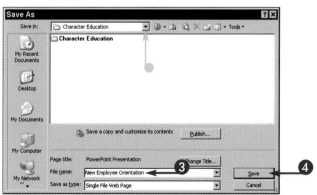

# Publish a Web Presentation

When you publish a Web presentation, make certain your settings are adjusted to show which slides to include and whether to display speaker notes as a way to give additional information to those viewing the presentation. By specifying an online location, you essentially post your presentation to that site.

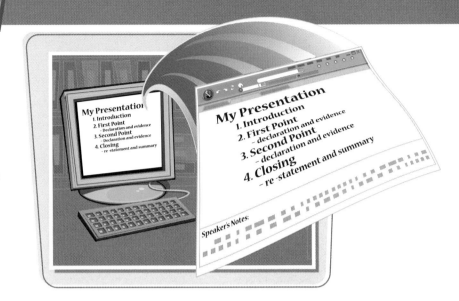

## Publish a Web Presentation

① Click **File**.

② Click **Save as Web Page**.

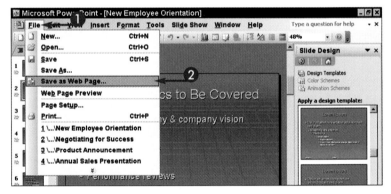

The Save As dialog box appears.

③ Click **Publish**.

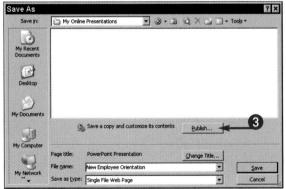

The Publish as Web Page dialog box appears.

④ Click **Slide number** (⊙ changes to ⊙) to publish only specified slides.

⑤ Type in the first slide and last slide numbers to include in the presentation.

● You can click to deselect the **Display speaker notes** option (☑ changes to ☐) to choose not to display speaker notes.

⑥ To publish to a Web site or other folder location, type the file path here or click **Browse**.

● To have the presentation open when you publish it, click the **Open Published Web Page in Browser** option (☐ changes to ☑).

⑦ Click **Publish**.

Your presentation opens in a Web page browser.

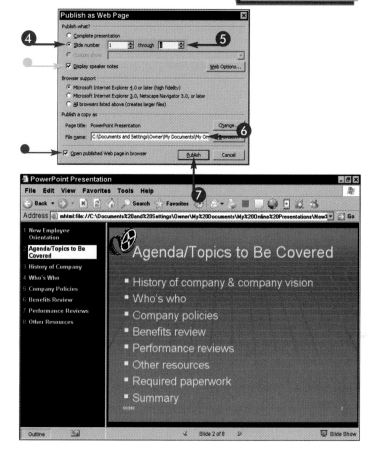

TIPS

**I created a custom show and want to publish it. How do I go about it?**

If you have saved custom shows, when you open the Publish as Web Page dialog box the **Custom show** option is available. Click that option (⊙ changes to ⊙) and select the Custom Show you want to use from the list. For more on saving a custom show, see Chapter 11.

**How do I change the title of the presentation that appears at the top of the browser window?**

In the Save As dialog box, before you click **Publish**, click **Change Title**, type a presentation name, and then click **OK**. Then proceed with publishing the presentation.

# Set Up Web Browser Support

Different Web browsers display information differently. For example, earlier versions of Internet Explorer cannot display some graphics formats accurately.

**If you know which browsers your audience is likely to be using, by selecting which browsers to support, you ensure that the presentation display is optimum for most people.**

## Set Up Web Browser Support

**1** With the Save As dialog box displayed, click **Publish**.

***Note:*** *See the section "Save a Presentation as a Web Page" to display the Save As dialog box.*

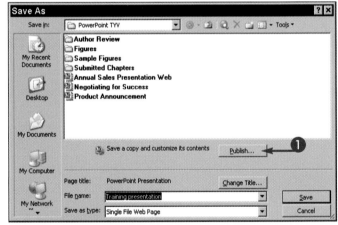

The Publish as Web Page dialog box appears.

**2** Click the browser you expect most of your viewers to use (○ changes to ⊙).

**3** Make any other settings for publishing your presentation.

***Note:*** *See the section "Publish a Web Presentation" for more about settings.*

**4** Click **Publish**.

PowerPoint saves the presentation and displays it in your Web browser.

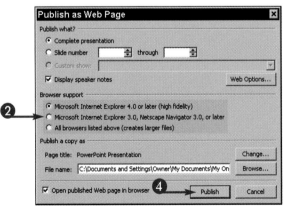

When you publish a presentation to the Web it is viewed in a browser. When you access the presentation, it offers certain tools you can use to move from slide to slide.

**You can use these tools yourself to preview your Web presentation to make sure everything is just as you want it to be. The following steps work whether you are viewing an online presentation or just previewing it.**

## Navigate a Presentation in a Browser

**①** Click **File**.

**②** Click **Web Page Preview**.

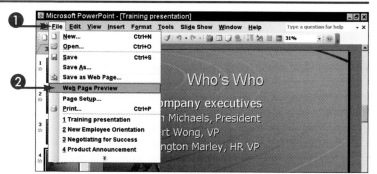

The presentation appears in a browser window.

**③** Click these arrows to move forward (⊡) or backward (⊡) one slide at a time.

**④** Click any slide title to move to that slide.

**⑤** Click **Expand/Collapse Outline** (⊡) to show more or less of the presentation outline.

**⑥** Click **Slide Show** to display the presentation in Full Screen Slide Show format.

You can press **Esc** to exit Full Screen mode.

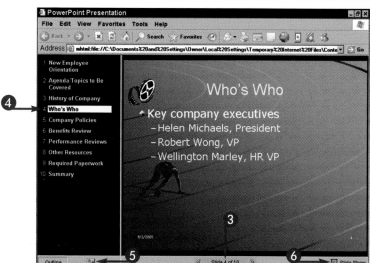

# Specify Fonts for Web Presentations

PowerPoint lets you use fonts that are installed with it, but sometimes those fonts are not available when people view a presentation online. You can set which fonts to use in a Web presentation by default. You can choose from proportional and fixed-width fonts.

*Proportional* fonts allow letters to use variable space; for example, the letter *l* uses less horizontal space than the letter *m*. With *fixed-width* fonts, every letter takes up a set amount of space.

## Specify Fonts for Web Presentations

① Click **File**.

② Click **Save as Web Page**.

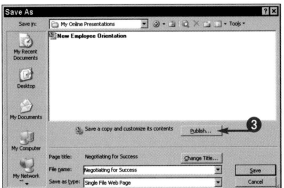

The Save As dialog box appears.

③ Click **Publish**.

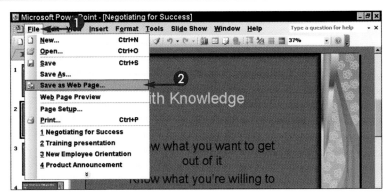

The Publish as Web Page dialog box appears.

④ Click **Web Options**.

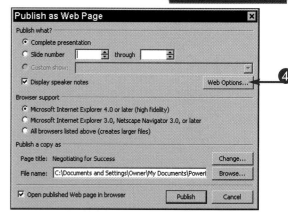

The Web Options dialog box appears.

⑤ Click the **Fonts** tab.

⑥ Click ▾ and select either a proportional or fixed-width font.

⑦ Click ▾ and select the font size for the chosen font.

⑧ Click **OK**.

The default font settings are saved and you return to the Publish as Web Page dialog box.

⑨ Click **Publish**.

PowerPoint publishes the page with your font choice.

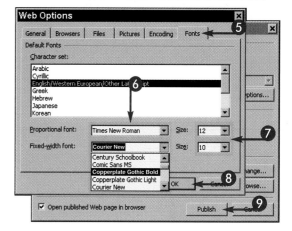

**TIPS**

**I am not sure whether to use a proportional or fixed-width font. What are the pros and cons of each?**

You should set a default for both. If a browser cannot recognize a font in your presentation, it uses the specified proportional or fixed-width fonts. By selecting a default font for each of these that most closely resembles fonts in your presentation, you ensure that your presentation looks as close as possible to your design.

**Do you have any advice about which fonts are most likely to be readable by most browsers?**

There are four fonts that are included in Microsoft Windows, and people with Windows-based computers are likely to have a Windows-based browser that can make use of them. Try using Times New Roman, Arial, Symbol, or Courier. Most browsers have no problem reading these.

# Customize Colors for Web Presentations

An online presentation uses a black Outline and Notes pane with white text by default. In addition, the slide background is black. You can change this setting to match your presentation colors, or use white with black text or the colors a user has set for his browser. You can also use your presentation's accent color for text.

## Customize Colors for Web Presentations

**1** Click **File**.

**2** Click **Save as Web Page**.

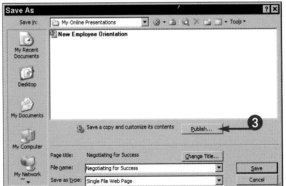

The Save As dialog box appears.

**3** Click **Publish**.

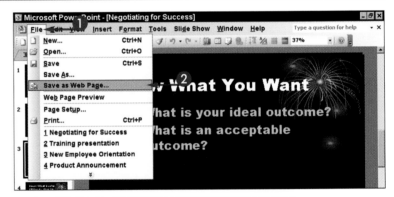

The Publish as Web Page dialog box appears.

④ Click **Web Options**.

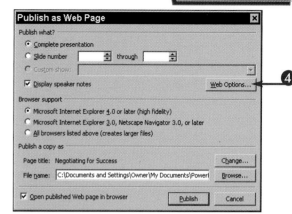

The Web Options dialog box appears with the General tab displayed.

⑤ If Add Slide Navigation Controls is not selected, click to select it (☐ changes to ☑).

⑥ Click here and select a color scheme.

⑦ Click **OK** to return to the Publish as Web Page dialog box.

⑧ Click **Publish**.

PowerPoint publishes the presentation with the selected colors.

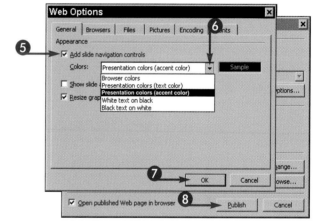

**TIPS**

### How do I prevent the Outline pane from appearing in my Web presentation?

You can do one of two things. In the Web Options dialog box used in the above steps, deselect the **Add Slide Navigation Controls** option (☐ changes to ☑). The second option is to make sure people run the show in Slide Show mode. The latter is probably a better option because it provides the option of using the navigation tools.

### How do I know what my presentation accent color is?

When you make this selection from the Colors list in the Web Options dialog box, the Sample box displays text in the accent color with the presentation background behind it. You can also see other choices previewed for you here before you make your final selection and publish the presentation.

# Finalize and Make a Presentation

Before you present your PowerPoint slide show, be sure you get all the input you need to make it final. You should also understand the tools available to you to make things flow smoothly during your presentation.

# Send a Presentation for Review

Often you find that you either want or are required to get somebody else's feedback on your slides before you give your presentation. This second opinion is a good idea because someone not close to the presentation can spot errors you have missed or suggest improvements.

**When somebody receives a file for review, changes are tracked so you can clearly see what has been changed. The person sends the file back via e-mail and you can accept or reject changes.**

**SEND A FILE FOR REVIEW**

① Click **File**.

② Click **Send To**.

③ Click **Mail Recipient (for Review)**.

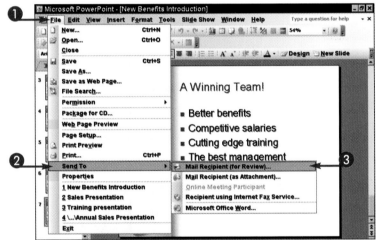

An e-mail message form appears.

④ Type the recipient's e-mail address.

⑤ Click here to edit or type additional text for the message.

⑥ Click **Send**.

PowerPoint sends the message with the presentation attached.

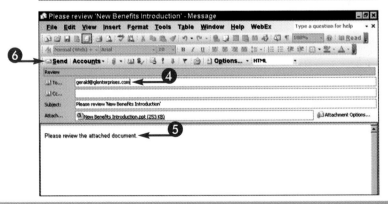

## OPEN A REVIEWED FILE

**1** When you receive a file back from a reviewer, open it.

**Note:** *If PowerPoint asks if you want to save or open the presentation, click* **Open**.

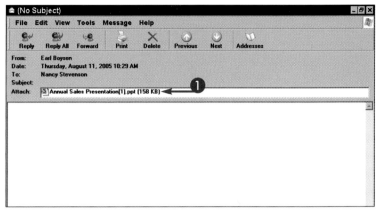

The Microsoft Office PowerPoint dialog box appears.

**Note:** *You can also download the attachment to your computer and open it using the method described in Chapter 2.*

**2** Click **Yes**.

Changes merge into your presentation.

The presentation opens with the Reviewing toolbar displayed.

**Note:** *See the section, "Review Changes to Your Presentation," to find out about using the Reviewing toolbar and task pane.*

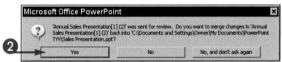

---

**TIPS**

**When I send a presentation for review, what will the recipient see when he opens it?**

The presentation looks just like the one you sent; however, it opens in PowerPoint with the Reviewing toolbar displayed. The recipient can click **Reply with Changes** on that toolbar to open an e-mail form. When you receive the e-mail back, a message says that the presentation was reviewed and the changed presentation is attached. All changes are automatically tracked. See the section "Review Changes to Your Presentation" for more about this.

**What happens if I choose the option on the Send To menu Mail Recipient (as Attachment) instead of Mail Recipient (for Review)?**

The presentation is sent to the person's e-mail inbox, however when he or she opens it, the Reviewing feature is not active. The person can manually display the Reviewing toolbar, but the only feature available is the comment feature. You cannot view changes in the returned file.

# Review Changes to Your Presentation

When you send a presentation to others for review, any changes they make are automatically tracked. When somebody sends the file back to you, you can review the changes and decide to incorporate them or reject them using the Reviewing toolbar and Reviewing task pane. You can accept or reject each change or act on inserted comments.

**The Compare and Merge Presentations feature allows you to see all the changes that others have made. This feature calls out changes by showing added text, deletions, and formatting changes.**

Review Changes to Your Presentation

① Open a presentation returned to you via e-mail.

*Note: See the section "Send a Presentation for Review" to open a presentation returned via e-mail.*

The presentation appears with the Reviewing toolbar and Revisions task pane displayed.

② Hold your mouse over a change marker.

● A detailed listing of changes appears.

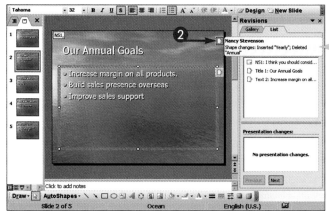

③ Click a slide change in the Revisions Task pane.

④ Click here and select **Apply**.

The change is accepted and a check mark appears by the change marker and in the Revisions Task pane.

● To accept all changes, you can click **Apply All Changes to the Current Slide** or **Apply All Changes to the Presentation**.

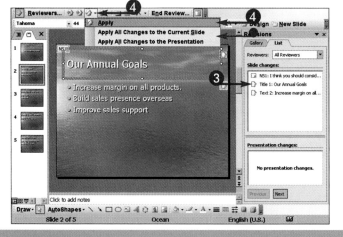

⑤ Hold your mouse over a comment.

● A comment window appears.

To delete a comment, you can right-click it and then click **Delete Comment**.

⑥ When you finish reviewing changes, click **End Review**.

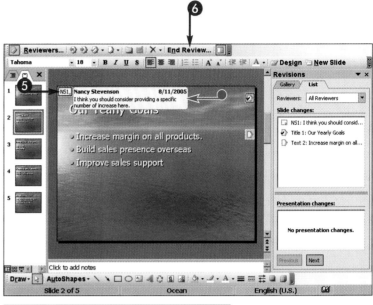

A dialog box appears to confirm you want to end the review.

⑦ Click **Yes**.

The dialog box closes and the review ends.

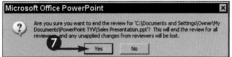

# Get Ready to Present

A successful live presentation requires solid content, good design, and a prepared presenter. Preparing to make a presentation involves double-checking your presentation for problems and getting yourself comfortable with your material and presentation environment.

### Check Your Presentation for Errors

There is nothing more embarrassing than displaying a slide in front of an audience only to find that your company's name is misspelled. Checking your slides for details such as spelling, grammatical usage, and typos can save you a lot of embarrassment when it is show time. Print the presentation outline to review the text so you are not distracted by design elements. Also, have somebody else who is not as close to the presentation, review it. That person may catch errors you have missed.

### Rehearse, Rehearse, Rehearse!

Talking through your presentation several times before you give it in front of an audience makes you feel more comfortable with the material and your own presentation style. Rehearse in front of a mirror or a friend, or even record yourself with a videocamera or CD recorder and play the recording back. You can spot irritating mannerisms or expressions and try to avoid them.

### Verify Your Timing

If you have been allotted 20 minutes for your presentation and it times out in rehearsal at 40 minutes, you have a problem. Always check your timing and if you must, edit your presentation or change the pacing to fit the time you have. Use the Rehearse feature of PowerPoint to walk through your presentation and record the time you take to cover each slide. If the total for all slides is too long or too short, make the necessary changes. See Chapter 11 for more about rehearsing your show.

## Record a Narration

If you do not intend to do a live presentation, for example if the audience will view the presentation at a kiosk, consider recording a narration. Even if your slide content is well prepared and explains your points well, a human voice can add a dimension to any presentation and help keep viewers focused. See Chapter 11 for information about recording a narration.

## Know Your Presentation Space

If it is possible to visit your presentation location before the big day, do so. Knowing the size of the room, the acoustics, and the layout of the stage and audience seating can help you prepare. If the space is large, you may want to request a microphone. If the space is too bright for people to easily see the slides, you may request that blinds be closed before you begin. The last thing you need on your presentation day is a problem with the presentation space you could have avoided.

## Set Up Your Show

Be sure to check those all-important settings. See Chapter 11 to review these. You should set up ahead of time the format for the presentation — such as a live presentation versus one shown at a kiosk — which slides to include, monitors and resolution, and how you will control the advancement from slide to slide.

## Save Your Presentation for the Road

Your presentation does you no good sitting on your desktop in Boise when you are presenting in Chicago. You have to save a copy of the presentation — even if you are bringing your laptop along, bring a CD backup anyway. You should package the presentation to include the PowerPoint viewer in case you find yourself on a computer without PowerPoint installed. And you should package any files you may have inserted a hyperlink into, as well.

# Start and End a Show

When you create a presentation by entering text and graphic elements and animations on slides, you have only to switch to Slide Show view to run the show. You can end the show at any time or wait for it to reach the end.

**After you move through the entire presentation, a black screen appears after the last slide with a note telling you to click your mouse to return to Normal view.**

## START A SHOW

**①** Click **Slide Show** (🖵).

The slide show starts with the currently selected slide.

*Note: To start from the beginning, select the first slide in the presentation before starting the show.*

## END A SHOW

**①** To end the show before you reach the last slide, click the **Slide Show Menu** icon (▭) on the presentation toolbar.

**②** Click **End Show**.

You return to Normal view.

You can also press Esc to end the show at any time.

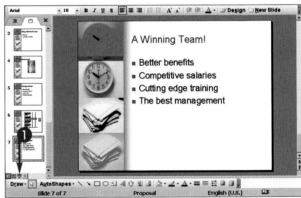

224

There are several options for moving from slide to slide during a presentation. You can use a shortcut menu and onscreen tools to move through a presentation given by a speaker. You can also use your right and left keyboard arrows to move forward and backward.

**If you have set up the show for an individual to browse, PowerPoint does not offer as many options for navigation. Viewers can use a scrollbar or the right and left arrow keys on a keyboard to move through the presentation.**

## Navigate Among Slides

① With a presentation in Slide Show view, move your mouse.

The Presentation toolbar appears.

② Click the right arrow (⬜) on the Presentation toolbar to move to the next slide.

*Note: See the section "Start and End a Show" to select Slide Show view.*

③ Click ⬜.

④ Click **Previous**.

PowerPoint displays the previous slide.

⑤ Click ⬜.

⑥ Click **Go to Slide**.

⑦ Click a slide title.

PowerPoint displays the slide you selected.

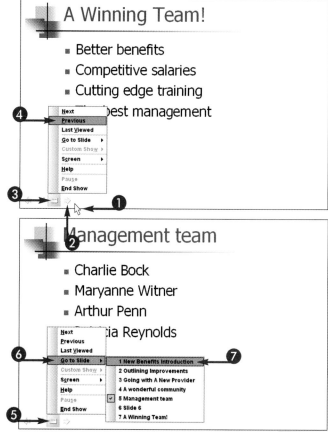

# Display a Black or White Screen

Before a presentation begins you may want to start the show but not display the title slide until you are ready. In this case you can turn the slide show screen entirely black or entirely white.

**You may also want to use this feature if you stop during the presentation for a discussion and find the slide content distracting to your audience.**

**1** With a slide show running, click ▢ on the presentation toolbar.

**Note:** *See the section "Start and End a Show" to select Slide Show view. See the section "Navigate Among Slides" to display the presentation toolbar.*

**2** Click **Screen**.

**3** Click **Black Screen** or **White Screen**.

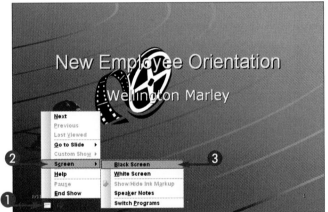

The screen turns completely black or white, depending on your choice but the presentation toolbar remains.

**4** Click the screen.

You return to the colored version of the presentation.

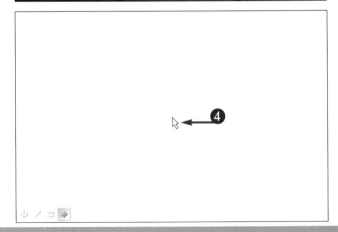

You can add speaker notes in the Notes pane of Normal view. These notes help you remember the details or background information about the bullet points on a slide.

You can display speaker notes during a presentation, and you can even take notes during the presentation. For example, sometimes during a presentation somebody brings up a point or you get an idea you want to add to your speaker notes for the next time you give the presentation.

## Add Speaker Notes

1 With a slide show running, click ⬚.

**Note:** See the section "Start and End a Show" to select Slide Show view. See the section "Navigate Among Slides" to display the presentation toolbar.

2 Click **Screen**.

3 Click **Speaker Notes**.

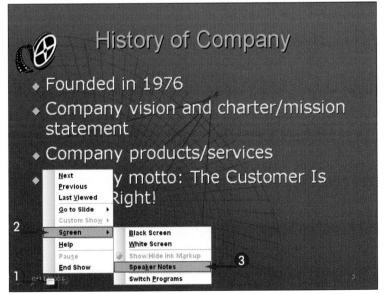

The Speaker Notes dialog box appears.

4 Type a note.

5 Click **Close**.

The Speaker Notes dialog box disappears.

Added text is now reflected in the Notes pane in Normal view.

# Using the Pointer

PowerPoint allows you to use a technology called ink, which allows you to draw on your screen during a presentation in freehand style. You use a pointer tool to do this. You can use ink to highlight or annotate a point.

**You can modify the format of the ink. For example, you can use a highlighter effect to highlight text, or a felt tip pen to circle or underline an object. You can also change the color of the ink.**

## Using the Pointer

**CHOOSE A POINTER STYLE**

① With a slide show running, click the **Pointer menu** icon (▱) on the presentation toolbar.

*Note: See the section "Start and End a Show" to select Slide Show view. See the section "Navigate Among Slides" to display the presentation toolbar.*

② Click a pointer style.

Styles include: **Ballpoint Pen**, which produces a thinner drawing line, **Felt Tip Pen**, which gives a little thicker drawing line, or **Highlighter**, which provides a transparent color wash.

*Note: Clicking arrow displays your mouse cursor arrow. You cannot draw any annotations with this option.*

③ Click the screen and drag your cursor.

Either a line or a highlight appears depending on your choice of pointer style.

## CHANGE INK COLOR

1 Click **Pointer menu** (☐) on the presentation toolbar.

2 Click **Ink Color**.

A color palette appears.

3 Click a color sample.

4 Click the screen and drag your mouse to write or draw an annotation.

The annotation appears in the new ink color.

---

**TIPS**

**I drew a lot of annotations during the presentation but now I want to get rid of them. How do I do that?**

Use the Erase feature. Click ☐, and then click **Erase All Ink on Slide** to clear all annotations on the currently displayed slide. Or you can click **Eraser** on the Pointer menu, which turns on the Eraser tool. Now click and drag your cursor over only the annotations you want to erase. When you are done, click **Eraser** on the Pointer menu again to turn it off.

**I find having the mouse cursor arrow visible during the presentation distracting. Is there a way to turn it off?**

Yes. Again using the Pointer menu, click Pointer Options and then **Arrow Options**, and then click **Hidden**. This hides the arrow from view, however it also hides the presentation toolbar. To display the arrow again, you have to right-click to display the shortcut menu, click **Arrow Options**, and then click either **Automatic** or **Visible**.

# Save or Discard Annotations

If you use the pointer to draw ink annotations during a presentation, you may or may not want to keep them all. If you do find them useful you can save them. If you do not want them and do not want to use the Erase feature to remove them one by one, you can choose not to save any of them.

**You are offered the option of saving or not saving annotations at the end of the show or if you end the show at any point.**

① With a slide show running and annotations drawn on some slides, click ▭.

**Note:** *See the section "Start and End a Show" to select Slide Show view. See the section "Navigate Among Slides" to display the presentation toolbar.*

② Click **End Show**.

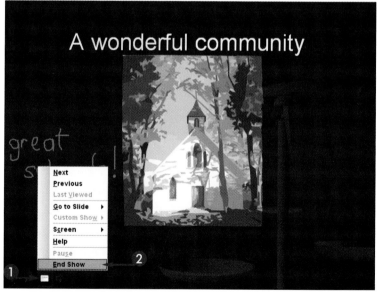

The Microsoft Office PowerPoint dialog box appears.

③ Click either **Discard** to discard annotations or **Keep** to keep annotations.

The dialog box closes and you return to Normal view.

**Note:** *If you keep annotations, you cannot erase them when you next run the show. To delete a saved annotation, click an annotation line in Normal view (▣) and use the Cut tool to delete it.*

If you need help running your show after your presentation has started, you do not want to stop the show and open PowerPoint Help.

**Luckily PowerPoint offers a single help screen with the most common presentation tips that you can display while running a show. This includes a list of shortcut keystrokes and procedures used to navigate the show and manage many of the presentation features, such as pointer options.**

## Display Slide Show Help

① With a slide show running, click 🔲.

**Note:** See the section "Start and End a Show" to select Slide Show view. See the section "Navigate Among Slides" to display the presentation toolbar.

② Click **Help**.

The Help window appears.

③ Look up the shortcut on the left to perform the procedure you want, which is listed on the right.

④ Click **OK**.

The Help window closes.

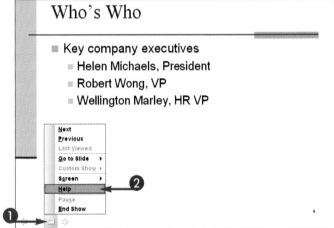

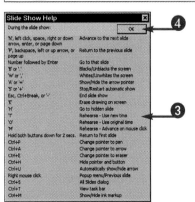

# CHAPTER 5

# Customizing PowerPoint

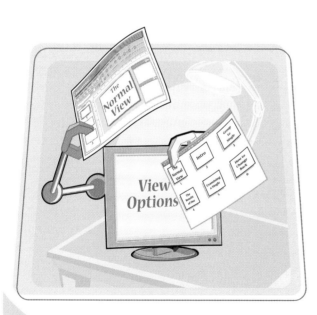

PowerPoint is a powerful tool, and it becomes even more powerful when you know how to customize it to work the way you need it to. You can make various settings that streamline the way you use PowerPoint.

# Modify PowerPoint File Properties

When you create a PowerPoint file you create a set of statistics about it such as the author name and date created. You can customize these file properties, changing some or adding others.

**For example, you may want to add your department name or a telephone number to the file properties so that somebody who receives it knows how to track you down. You can also add keywords that help you search for the file if you should forget the file name.**

① Click **File**.

② Click **Properties**.

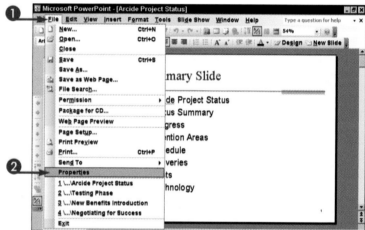

The Properties dialog box appears.

③ Click the **Summary** tab.

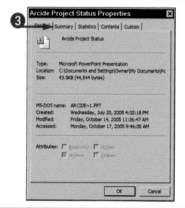

**4** Click in any field and type to edit or add information.

*Note: The name of the logged in computer user is entered automatically as the Author, but you can change that here.*

**5** Click the **Custom** tab.

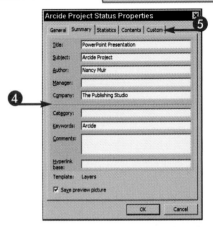

**6** Click an item in the Name list to add.

**7** Click here and select a type of data from the list.

**8** Type in the Value field.

**9** Click **Add**.

The information is added to the file custom properties.

**10** Click **OK**.

The dialog box closes and new properties are saved.

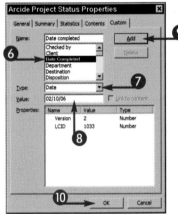

 **TIPS**

**What do I use the other tabs of the Properties dialog box for?**
These tabs summarize data about your file which is generated automatically. For example, the **General** tab tells you the location where the file is stored on your computer; the file size; dates created, last accessed, or modified; and file attributes such as read only. The **Statistics** tab displays information, such as the number of paragraphs, words, and notes in the presentation. The **Content** tab gives an overview of presentation contents such as the slide design used, slide titles, and fonts used.

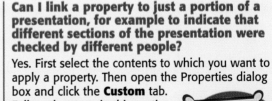

**Can I link a property to just a portion of a presentation, for example to indicate that different sections of the presentation were checked by different people?**
Yes. First select the contents to which you want to apply a property. Then open the Properties dialog box and click the **Custom** tab. Follow the steps in this section to add a custom property, and click the **Link to content** option (☐ changes to ☑). Whatever property you chose is now linked to the selected content in the presentation.

# Customize Save Options

If you are wise you save your presentations on a regular basis so you do not lose any data. You can set up PowerPoint to save things the way you prefer, which can make all that saving faster and easier. For example, you can change the default saved file format or set up a default location to which to save files.

You can also make settings that control the AutoRecover feature. AutoRecover saves any changes you have made on a regular interval that you can set. If your computer crashes, AutoRecover might be able to offer you a reasonably recent version of your document when you start up again.

## Customize Save Options

① Click **Tools**.

② Click **Options**.

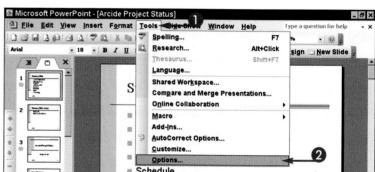

The Options dialog box appears.

③ Click the **Save** tab.

The Save tab appears.

④ Click a Save option (☐ changes to ☑).

You can click options to only save changes since you last saved the file, to display the Properties dialog box when you first save a file, to set how frequently your file automatically saves, or to revert to a file format compatible with earlier versions of Microsoft Graph.

⑤ Click here and select a different default file format to use when saving files.

⑥ Type the default location to save files to.

⑦ Click the **Embed TrueType fonts** option (☐ changes to ☑) to embed True Type fonts when saving a file.

Two options become available.

⑧ Click the option you prefer (◯ changes to ◉) to embed only used characters or all characters.

⑨ Click **OK**.

The dialog box closes and Save options are saved.

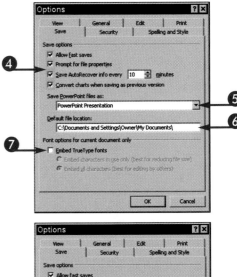

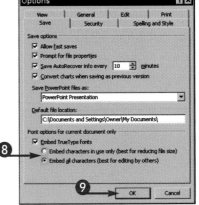

**TIPS**

**What are the pros and cons of having the AutoRecover feature make frequent saves?**

AutoRecover is a kind of safety net for your data. This feature saves changes to your file at regular intervals. If your system crashes and you have not saved your file, an AutoRecover version may contain more of your changes so you can avoid having to do all your work over again. However AutoRecover can cause your system to pause for a second or two while it runs so you should not set it to run every minute or so. It is a good idea to leave AutoRecover set between the default 10 minutes and 5 minutes to avoid data loss.

**What are TrueType fonts and why would I want to embed them in a presentation?**

TrueType fonts are font families that come with Windows and Microsoft Office. Four base fonts — Times New Roman, Arial, Symbol, and Courier New — are available to all Windows users automatically. Others, such as Book Angiqua or Garamond, are not available to every computer. If you use these in a presentation and do not embed them and somebody viewing the presentation does not have those fonts on that computer, PowerPoint may replace them with a base font, which may throw off your presentation design.

You can change what elements display in PowerPoint views and when running a slide show. You can also set up a default view to use, such as the Outline tab only in Normal view, or Slide Sorter view.

**Although you can modify the view at any time using View menu commands, having your presentations default to the view you use most often can save you time. Being able to modify how and when items appear when running a slide show can make your presentations more efficient.**

## Modify View Options

① Click **Tools**.

② Click **Options**.

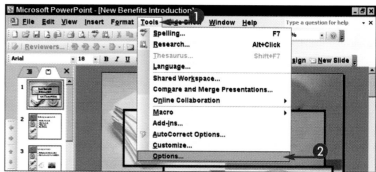

The Options dialog box appears.

③ Click the **View** tab.

The View tab appears.

**4** Click any of the Show options (☑ changes to ☐) to remove an element from the Normal or Slide Sorter view.

**5** Click any of the Slide Show options (☑ changes to ☐) to change what displays when running a show.

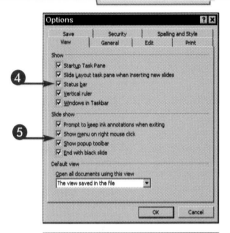

**6** Click here and select a default view.

**7** Click **OK**.

The dialog box closes and your new settings are saved.

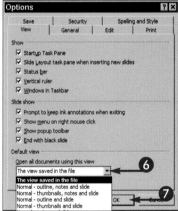

**What is the benefit to displaying the Slide Layout task pane when I insert a new slide?**

When you insert a new slide, PowerPoint inserts it with the Title and Text layout by default. Quite often you may want to change the layout, perhaps to one with a content placeholder or two side by side bullet lists. Having the Layout task pane appear automatically saves you the trouble of displaying it frequently when you are building a new presentation.

**If I change the setting for PowerPoint to prompt me to save annotations on exiting a presentation, is there any other way for me to save them?**

No. The only method you can use to save annotations is via the dialog box that appears to prompt you to save them. With that option deselected (☑ changes to ☐) in the **View** tab of the Options dialog box, you can no longer save annotations.

You can change how various editing tools work. For example, you can modify how cutting and pasting, text selection, and the Undo feature perform. You can also enable or disable certain features that are new to PowerPoint 2003.

**One feature available in the most recent Office products that you can control is the use of smart tags. Smart tags display a small icon that offers a menu of options when you perform actions, such as pasting a cut or copied object or text.**

## Change Editing Settings

**①** Click **Tools**.

**②** Click **Options**.

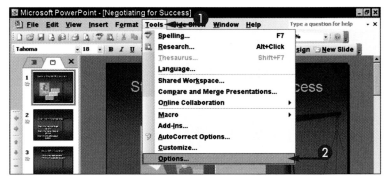

The Options dialog box appears.

**③** Click the **Edit** tab.

The Edit tab appears.

④ Click any of the following options (☐ changes to ☑).

● Cut and Paste options control the use of smart tags when pasting text or objects.

● Text options offer automatic word selection and drag-and-drop editing features for moving text around a presentation outline.

● The Charts setting, when active, automatically applies the current slide design font to be used in new charts.

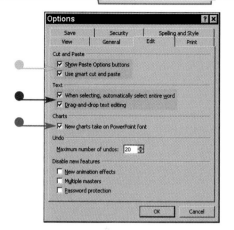

⑤ Click to raise or lower the maximum number of Undo actions.

⑥ Click (☐ change to ☑) to enable any new features in PowerPoint 2003.

⑦ Click **OK**.

The dialog box closes and any changed settings are saved.

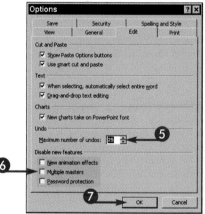
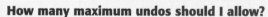

 TIPS

### What is the difference between the Paste Options button and smart cut and paste?
The Paste Options button appears below a pasted object. It offers formatting options such as retaining the original source formatting or using design template formatting in the destination file or slide. A smart tag function displays an indicator in the form of a wavy line that tells you there are some actions you can perform on certain types of data, which you would normally use another program for. When you move your cursor over the indicator, a button appears you can click it to access options.

### How many maximum undos should I allow?
Undos work sequentially through the last actions you have taken. The default undo option is 20 and that is probably about right. If you have to perform the undo function more than 20 times it is most likely not worth your time to use it. One option is to go back and manually reconstruct the way things were before your actions, or to simply not save the work you have done in the file since your last save.

# Work with Print Options

PowerPoint has several options for printing your presentation that you can set in the Options dialog box. You can modify the way your printer handles fonts and inserted graphics resolution, for example.

**You can also override default printer settings by specifying print settings for this document only. By making these settings in the Options dialog box, you avoid changing print settings for all documents you print during this session of PowerPoint.**

## Work with Print Options

① Click **Tools**.

② Click **Options**.

The Options dialog box appears.

③ Click the **Print** tab.

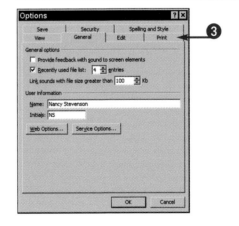

④ Click (☐ changes to ☑) to select various print options.

● The **Background printing** option allows you to continue to work in PowerPoint while your document prints.

● The **Print TrueType fonts as graphics** option downloads fonts to your printer, which can speed up printing.

● The **Print inserted objects at printer resolution** option overrides the inserted object resolution settings in favor of your printer's setting.

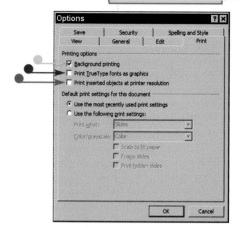

⑤ Click the **Use the following print settings** option (◌ changes to ⦿) to override default print settings.

The rest of the fields become available.

⑥ Click here and select an item to print.

⑦ Click here and select which color option to use.

**Note:** *See Chapter 12 for more about Printing preferences.*

⑧ Click **OK**.

The dialog box closes and your settings are saved.

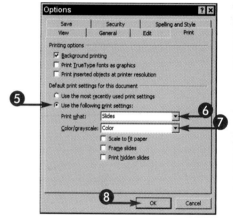

**TIPS**

**My Options dialog box does not make the Print TrueType fonts as graphics option available. Why?**

This option is only available if your printer model supports it. Laser printers typically support the option, but dot matrix and plotters often do not. With this setting enabled (☐ changes to ☑), font files are actually downloaded to reside in your printer, which can take up a lot of printer memory. In some cases even though this option may be available, your printer does not print properly. If that happens, disabling this feature (☑ changes to ☐) may solve the problem.

**My printer prints slowly. Any suggestions about how to fix this?**

Try a couple of things. Enabling the **Background Printing** option (☐ changes to ☑) can slow down your printer, so you may try turning that feature off. Also, using fonts that are installed in your printer — called *resident fonts* — can be faster than downloading fonts from your computer. Check your printer manual to see what resident fonts it may contain that suit your presentation.

# Change AutoCorrect Settings

With AutoCorrect you can have PowerPoint correct common typing or spelling errors. You can also add settings to correct your own poor habits, such as typing "oin" when you meant to type "ion" in various words.

You may want to change some of the default AutoCorrect settings. For example if you often have a need to use the notation (c) and do not want it automatically changed to the copyright symbol, ©, you can remove that AutoCorrect setting.

Change AutoCorrect Settings

① Click **Tools**.

② Click **AutoCorrect Options**.

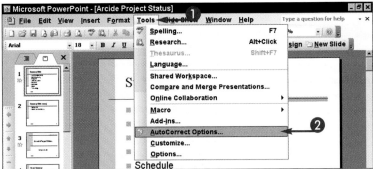

The AutoCorrect dialog box appears.

● If the AutoCorrect tab does not display, click it.

③ Click to turn off any of the standard AutoCorrect features (☑ changes to ☐).

● You can type a term into the Replace field, and a term with which to replace it in the With field and then click **Add** to have PowerPoint automatically replace a typed word.

④ Click **Exceptions**.

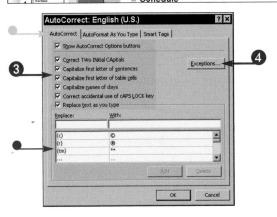

The Exceptions dialog box appears with the First Letter tab displayed.

**5** Type a term in the Don't Capitalize After field.

**6** Click **Add**.

The term is added to the list.

**7** Click the **INitial CAps** tab.

**8** Type a term with acceptable initial caps.

**9** Click **Add**.

**10** Click **OK**.

You return to the AutoCorrect dialog box.

**11** Click **OK**.

The dialog box closes and your AutoCorrect changes are saved.

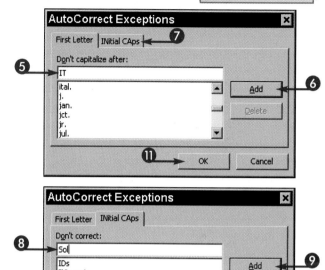

**TIPS**

**I have a few terms I always type in full caps, but sometimes PowerPoint changes the words to lowercase. Why?**

You are probably using the Caps Lock key to type these words. AutoCorrect has a setting that corrects accidental use of the Caps Lock key. Essentially when you begin to type text within a sentence in full caps, PowerPoint changes the word to lowercase or intial caps. To turn this feature off, display the AutoCorrect dialog box and click the **Correct accidential use of cAPS LOCK key** option (☑ changes to ☐). Click **OK** and you should no longer have the problem.

**Occasionally I type the term 'acn' which is an acronym we use in my company. AutoCorrect changes it to 'can'. I would rather not delete that AutoCorrect setting, as it comes in handy sometimes. Any other ideas?**

For a one-time or occasional AutoCorrection that you do not want to keep, use the Undo feature. A keyboard shortcut that comes in handy is Ctrl + Z . After typing **acn**, when AutoCorrect changes it, just press Ctrl + Z and it changes back.

# Change AutoFormat and Smart Tag Settings

AutoFormat works similarly to AutoCorrect, except that it corrects formatting of text rather than text itself. AutoFormat controls settings such as automatically changing a list of items to a numbered list or changing two hyphens to a dash.

**Smart Tags provide a way to quickly perform certain types of actions on certain types of text. If you enable Smart Tags, PowerPoint underlines certain text and displays a Smart Tags Action button you can activate to display a list of possible actions.**

Change AutoFormat and Smart Tag Settings

**CHANGE AUTOFORMAT SETTINGS**

① Click **Tools**.

② Click **AutoCorrect Options**.

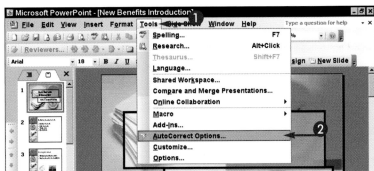

The AutoCorrect dialog box appears.

③ Click the **AutoFormat As You Type** tab.

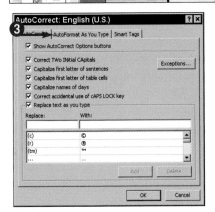

④ Click any field (☑ changes to ☐) to turn off an AutoFormat setting.

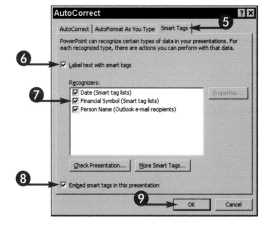

**ENABLE SMART TAGS**

⑤ Click the Smart Tags tab.

⑥ Click the **Label text with smart tags** option (☐ changes to ☑).

The Recognizers options become available.

⑦ Click to disable any of these types of smart tags (☑ changes to ☐).

⑧ Click to embed smart tags in the presentation (☐ changes to ☑).

*Note: Smart tags are not automatically visible to others who look at the presentation; embedding them makes them available to anybody looking at your file.*

⑨ Click **OK**.

The dialog box closes and your new settings are saved.

 **TIPS**

**Smart Tags are cool. Are there others available?**
In the AutoCorrect dialog box, on the Smart Tags tab, click **More Smart Tags**. You are taken to the Microsoft Office Online page with a list of available Smart Tags you can download. Third parties, not Microsoft, provide these, but they are free. Some require that you restart your computer before the new tag becomes available to you.

**Every time I type an online address in a document, PowerPoint changes it to a link. How can I avoid that?**
That is the result of an AutoFormat setting. Open the AutoCorrect dialog box and click the **AutoFormat As You Type** tab. Click to deselect **Internet and network paths with hyperlinks** option (☑ changes to ☐). Click **OK** and your new setting is saved.

# Customize Menus

Menus are an alternate way to access many functions you find on toolbars. In some cases a menu is the only way to access a function. You can customize menus to rearrange commands, add commands, or delete commands.

**You can even change the icon that appears next to a menu command, or set your menus to use text only. If you make changes to menus and then decide you want to go back to the default menu style, you can reset menus one by one or all at once.**

**①** Click **View**.

**②** Click **Toolbars.**

**③** Click **Customize.**

The Customize dialog box appears.

**④** Click the **Commands** tab.

**⑤** Click a menu category.

The commands currently available on that menu appear in the list on the right.

**⑥** Click **Rearrange Commands**.

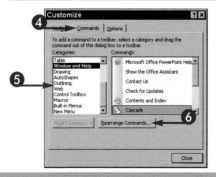

The Rearrange Commands dialog box appears.

**7** Click to add, delete, move up, or move down the command in the menu.

**8** Click **Modify Selection** and select another image for the command from the menu that appears.

You can delete the command.

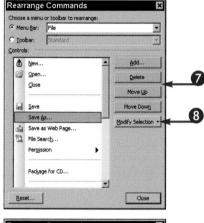

**9** Click **Close** in the Rearrange Commands dialog box.

**10** Click **Close** in the Customize dialog box.

Both dialog boxes close and your menu changes are saved.

**Somebody using my computer while I was on vacation reset the image for a command I use all the time to a frown symbol and it annoys me. How do I get it back the way it was?**

In the Rearrange Commands dialog box select the command. Click **Modify Selection**, and then click **Reset Button Image**. Click **Close** twice, and the image next to the command on the menu changes back to the default.

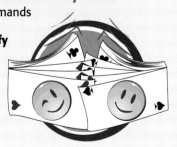

**Is there a way to rename a menu?**

Yes. In the Rearrange Commands dialog box select the command. Click **Modify Selection** and in the Name field type a new name, and then click **Close** twice. Be careful about renaming built-in menus, though. Somebody else using your computer may have trouble finding what he or she needs!

# Create a New Toolbar

Toolbars are something you use all the time to get your work done. However, the preset toolbars that come with PowerPoint do not necessarily provide the tools you use most often. You can create new toolbars, assembling the tools you use most often in one place or creating specialized sets of tools.

**If you no longer need a toolbar you can delete it, however, it is suggested that you not delete standard PowerPoint toolbars. You can also modify toolbars to support the way you work. For more on modifying toolbars, see the section "Modify a Toolbar."**

## Create a New Toolbar

① Click **View**.

② Click **Toolbars.**

③ Click **Customize.**

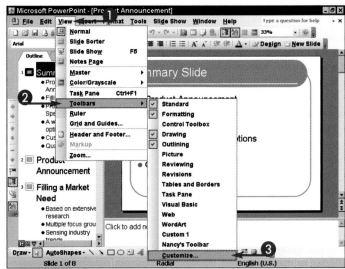

The Customize dialog box appears.

④ Click **New**.

The New Toolbar dialog box appears.

⑤ Type a name for the toolbar.

⑥ Click **OK**.

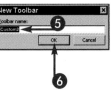

● A blank, floating toolbar appears.

⑦ Click the **Commands** tab.

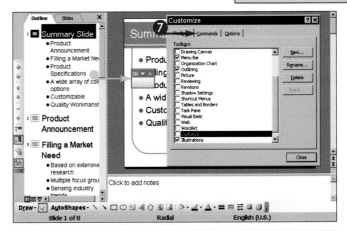

⑧ Click a command category.

⑨ Click a command and drag it to the new toolbar.

⑩ When you have dragged all the commands you want to your toolbar, click **Close**.

The dialog box closes and your new toolbar remains displayed.

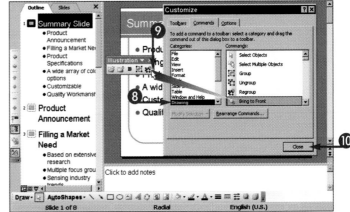

**TIPS**

**I created a new toolbar but I want to divide the sets of tool buttons into categories. Can I do that?**

Yes. Select the button that you want to place a divider to the right of. Click the **Command** tab of the Customize dialog box. Click **Modify Selection** and then click the **Begin a Group** command on the list. A small divider line appears between that button and the one next to it. Repeat this for each group you want to create.

**Once I create a toolbar, how do I display it?**

You display your custom toolbar just as you display any toolbar. Click **View**, click **Toolbars**, and click the toolbar name in the list that appears. Alternately, you can right-click the toolbar area, outside of any displayed toolbar, and click the toolbar name on the list that appears.

You can modify existing toolbars to add or remove buttons from them using toolbar options. You may do this because a button you use all the time is not available by default on the toolbar.

**On the other hand, toolbars with a great many buttons displayed can make it hard to find the ones you use most often. In that case, you can remove buttons from view. Modifying toolbars in this fashion is easy to do, and can make you much more efficient.**

## Modify a Toolbar

① With a toolbar displayed click the Toolbar Options arrow ( ).

② Click **Add or Remove Buttons**.

③ Click the toolbar name.

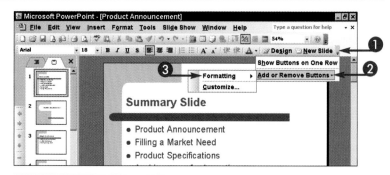

A list of buttons appears; those with checkmarks ( ) are currently shown on the toolbar.

④ Click a currently displayed button name to remove it.

⑤ Click a button not currently displayed to display it.

⑥ Click outside the menu.

The toolbar changes.

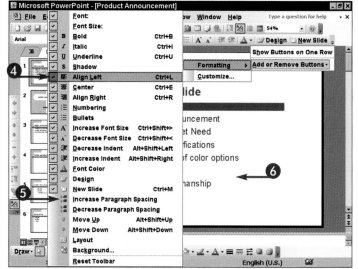

PowerPoint allows you to protect your files with a password. Once you set a password, nobody can open the file without entering it. This is useful for protecting highly confidential presentations.

**However, you should be careful about using a password. Once you set a password, if you forget it, you cannot open your file again!**

### Set a Password

1 Click **Tools.**

2 Click **Options**.

The Options dialog box appears.

● If necessary click the **Security** tab.

3 Type a password.

4 Click **OK**.

The dialog box closes and the password is set.

The next time you open the file, PowerPoint prompts you to enter the password.

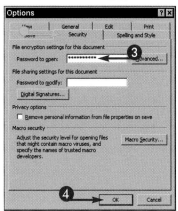

# Record and Play Back Macros

A macro is a feature you can use to record a series of actions that you perform frequently. You can then play back the macro to repeat the steps with just a few keystrokes. Macros can save you a lot of time.

For example, you may use a macro to insert multiple slides that use a non-default layout. Rather than individually inserting and changing the layout of each slide, you can run a macro that inserts, say, 4 or 5 such slides at a time.

**RECORD THE MACRO**

① Click **Tools**.

② Click **Macro**.

③ Click **Record New Macro**.

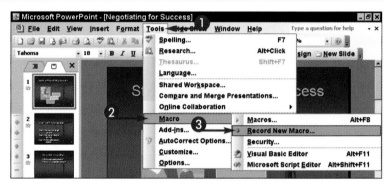

The Record Macro dialog box appears.

④ Type a name for the macro.

*Note: Macro names cannot contain spaces.*

⑤ Click **OK**.

The dialog box disappears and the macro begins recording.

⑥ Perform the actions you want to record.

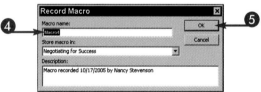

**7** Click **Tools**.

**8** Click **Macro**.

**9** Click **Stop Recording**.

**PLAY THE MACRO**

**10** Press `Alt` + `F8` .

The Macro dialog box appears.

**11** Click the macro.

**12** Click **Run**.

The macro plays back the steps you recorded.

**I made a mistake while recording the macro. Though I undid the mistake the action is still in the macro. Is there any way to edit it out?**

You have two options here. If it is not a lengthy procedure, you can just rerecord the macro. This is often your best option. If you find it too cumbersome to rerecord the macro, you can edit it. In the Macro dialog box, which you open by pressing `Alt` + `F8`, click the macro and click **Edit**. A word of warning: the macro is written in Visual Basic code. If you correct the code, for example changing "View" to "Tools" to change your menu selection, be careful not to change anything else inadvertently or the code may not work.

**I use one macro all the time. Is there a way to quickly run it without opening the Macro dialog box?**

Yes. You can add a macro to a toolbar. You have to have saved the file after creating the macro first. Then on the **Commands** tab of the Customize dialog box, click **Macros**. Click and drag the macro you want onto a toolbar, and then click **Close**. See the section "Create a New Toolbar" for more on opening the Customize dialog box.

# APPENDIX

# PowerPoint Keyboard Shortcuts

Many people find that using the keyboard to initiate commands is faster than using on screen menus. As you work with PowerPoint you may want to try out a few of these keyboard shortcuts yourself.

Keyboard shortcuts often consist of a combination of a key such as **Ctrl** or **Alt** and a number or letter key. For example, **Ctrl**+**V** pastes text from the Windows Clipboard into a document. In other cases you can use a single function key, such as **F6**, to perform an action.

# Keyboard Shortcuts for Common Tasks

There are many tasks you perform in PowerPoint no matter whether you focus on slide design, text entry, or presentation organization. Here are keyboard shortcuts for some of these common tasks.

## Common Tasks

| To Perform This Action | Press This |
| --- | --- |
| Move among panes in Normal view | `F6` |
| Switch between Slides and Outline tab | `Ctrl` + `Shift` + `Tab` |
| Select consecutive slides or objects | `Shift` +click |
| Select non-consecutive slides or objects | `Ctrl` +click |
| Display or hide grid | `Shift` + `F9` |
| Display or hide guides | `Alt` + `F9` |
| Select cursor one character to the right | `Shift` + → |
| Select cursor one character to the left | `Shift` + ← |
| Select cursor to end of word | `Ctrl` + `Shift` + → |
| Select cursor to beginning of word | `Ctrl` + `Shift` + ← |
| Select from insertion point to end of text in a field | `Shift` + `End` |
| Select all objects | `Ctrl` + `A` on Slides tab |
| Select all slides | `Ctrl` + `A` in Slide Sorter view |
| Select all text | `Ctrl` + `A` on Outline tab |
| Switch to next tab in dialog box | `Ctrl` + `Tab` |
| Switch to previous tab in dialog box | `Ctrl` + `Shift` + `Tab` |
| Move between options in drop-down list | ↓ , ↑ , → , ← |
| Check or clear a check box | `Spacebar` |
| Open a selected drop down list | `Alt` + ↓ |
| Close a selected drop-down list or cancel a command | `Esc` |

When your focus is on editing, performing tasks such as cutting and pasting or copying items, these shortcuts will come in handy.

## Edit Text and Objects Shortcuts

| To Perform This Action | Press This |
|---|---|
| Delete one word to the left of cursor | Ctrl + Backspace |
| Delete one word to the right of cursor | Ctrl + Delete |
| Cut selected item | Ctrl + X |
| Copy selected item | Ctrl + C |
| Paste cut or copied item | Ctrl + V |
| Undo last action | Ctrl + Z |
| Change font | Ctrl + Shift + F |
| Change font size | Ctrl + Shift + P |
| Increase font size | Ctrl + Shift + > |
| Decrease font size | Ctrl + Shift + < |
| Change letter case | Shift + F3 |
| Apply bold | Ctrl + B |
| Apply italic | Ctrl + I |
| Apply underline | Ctrl + U |
| Copy text format | Ctrl + Shift + C |
| Paste text format | Ctrl + Shift + V |

# Keyboard Shortcuts for Slide Show Presentations

When you are running your presentation several keyboard shortcuts make it easier to navigate your show.

## Slide Show Presentation Shortcuts

| To Perform This Action | Press This |
| --- | --- |
| Go to slide number | Number+ Enter |
| Erase annotations | E |
| Go to next animation | N , Enter , Page down , → or ↓ |
| Go to previous animation | P , Page up , ← or ↑ , Backspace |
| End slide show | Esc , Ctrl + Break |
| Go to first slide | 1 + Enter |
| View controls list | F1 |

If you are browsing a Web presentation, use these shortcuts to navigate the slides.

| Web Presentation Shortcuts | |
| --- | --- |
| *To Perform This Action* | *Press This* |
| Move through hyperlinks | Tab |
| Move back through hyperlinks | Shift + Tab |
| Initiate hyperlink | Enter |
| Go to next slide | Spacebar |
| Go to previous slide | Backspace |

# Keyboard Shortcuts for Sharing Presentations

You can share presentations for review via e-mail. The first item is performed from within PowerPoint; the other shortcuts work from your e-mail program with an e-mail header field active.

| E-mail Presentation Shortcuts | |
| --- | --- |
| *To Perform This Action* | *Press This* |
| Send presentation as e-mail message | Alt + S |
| Open Address Book | Ctrl + Shift + B |
| Check addresses against Address Book | Alt + K |
| Select the next field in the e-mail header | Tab |
| Select the previous field in the e-mail header | Shift + Tab |

Moving around the Help feature of PowerPoint using shortcuts gets you the answers you need much faster.

| Help Shortcuts | |
| --- | --- |
| *To Perform This Action* | *Press This* |
| Display Help | F1 |
| Move between Help and application | F6 |
| Select next Help item | Tab |
| Select previous Help item | Shift + Tab |
| Select next item in Table of Contents | ↑ |
| Select previous item in Table of Contents | ↓ |
| Move to previous task pane | Alt + ← |
| Move to next task pane | Alt + → |
| Open menu of options | Ctrl + Spacebar |
| Expand a list of topics | → |
| Collapse a list of topics | ← |
| Print the Help topic | Ctrl + P |
| Tile/untile Help window to application | Alt + U |

# APPENDIX B

## Online Resources

PowerPoint has a loyal following around the world. Many companies and individuals have created discussion forums, free graphics, Web publications and more that you will find of use. Some of these are free, and some require that you sign up for a membership or pay a fee, or take out a subscription.

The resources provided here help add punch to your presentations and make your PowerPoint experience more enjoyable.

**Several Web sites offer advice and tools to make your PowerPoint experience more interesting. Many of these sites offer training, tutorials, or advice free or for a fee.**

### KidzOnline

You can find this site at **www.kidzonline.org/TechTraining/ video.asp?UnitQry=PowerPoint**. This is a good site for kids who want to learn PowerPoint. Here you can find streaming videos and tips to help anybody use PowerPoint more effectively.

### Crystal Graphics

You can find this site at **www.crystalgraphics.com/powerpoint/ presentations.main.asp**. This site provides plug-ins that help make PowerPoint even more powerful. Their PowerPlugs add pizazz to transitions, video backgrounds, charts, and more.

### PowerPoint in the Classroom

If you work with PowerPoint training you may find this PowerPoint in the Classroom site at **www.actden.com/pp/** useful. There are helpful tutorials and teachers' guides on this interesting site.

### The PowerPoint FAQ

This site is at **www.rdpslides.com/pptfaq/**. The site answers many questions that may come up when you are learning PowerPoint. They offer several categories such as Tips, Techniques, and Tutorials and Troubleshooting for you to browse.

### A Bit Better Corporation

This site offers PowerPoint information at **www.bitbetter.com/powertips.htm**. Their tips and tricks are informative and useful.

# Sources for Templates and Graphics

The templates and graphics included with PowerPoint are great, but they are available to everybody creating a presentation in PowerPoint and can get stale. Find fresh graphics and templates to set your presentations apart at these sites and others.

## PixelMill

You can find this site at **www.pixelmill.com**. This site charges for its templates, including graphic decks and animated Flash movies. You can download a free sample and tutorial.

## PowerFinish

You can find this site at **www.powerfinish.com.** It offers 14,000 PowerPoint templates and presentations for sale. You can download your purchases to use them right away.

### Clipart.com

You can find this at **www.clipart.com/en/**. It offers a subscription-based service you can use to download collections of clip art to add pizazz to your presentations.

### All Free Original Clipart

This is a site that gives away its clip art. The address is **www.free-graphics.com/**. They have over 30,000 free clip art files, ranging from illustrations to animation files.

### BrainyBetty

This site is at **www.brainybetty.com.** It offers animations, backgrounds, and templates as well as PowerPoint tutorials and tips and tricks.

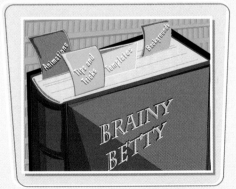

# Microsoft Resources

Microsoft itself offers lots of support for PowerPoint, including advice, additional templates, and graphics for free download. Remember you can also use the online features in both the Clip Art and New Presentation task panes to quickly access these sites.

### Microsoft Office Online

**office.microsoft.com/en-us/default.aspx** is where you go if you choose Microsoft Office Online in the Help menu. Here, you find advice, demos, discussion groups, and third-party software that adds functionality to PowerPoint.

### Microsoft Clip Art

Microsoft offers clip art beyond their included collections at **office.microsoft.com/clipart/default.aspx?lc=en-**. Clip art is divided into a few dozen categories including Abstract, Academic, Food, Sciences, and Travel. All this clip art is free, so enjoy!

## Microsoft Template Site

Microsoft's template site is at **office.microsoft.com/en-us/ templates/default.aspx**. Browse templates by categories such as Business and Legal or Education to find the one that is right for your presentation.

## Microsoft Discussion Groups

If you want to join PowerPoint related discussion groups, go to **www.microsoft.com/office/community/en-us/default.mspx**, the home of Microsoft discussion groups.

## Microsoft PowerPoint Certification

If you become really sharp in using PowerPoint and want to get certification as a PowerPoint user, go to **www.microsoft.com/ learning/** to sign up for certified testing. You can also find Web casts and Microsoft-hosted events through this site.

# Index

## Numbers and Symbols

3D effects, 132–133

## A

Action Button palette, 167
action buttons. *See also* animation schemes; hyperlinks; macros.
    inserting, 166–167
    overview, 157
advancing slides, 168, 171. *See also* transitions.
aligning drawings, 141. *See also* grids; guides; nudging objects.
All Free Original Clipart, 269
animation schemes. *See also* action buttons; macros.
    applying to slides, 158–159
    custom, 161–163
    definition, 156
    deleting, 165
    disabling, 179
    overview, 156–157
    previewing, 160
    pros and cons, 159
    reorganizing, 164
    repeating, 163
    timing, 163
annotations
    creating, 228–229
    discarding, 230
    prompt for save, 239
    saving, 230, 239
arranging windows, 25
AutoContent Wizard, 18–19
AutoCorrect. *See also* AutoFormat; Smart Tags.
    cAPS LOCK key option, 245
    customizing, 244–245
    overriding one-time occurrences, 245
AutoFormat, 246–247. *See also* AutoCorrect; Smart Tags.
AutoFormat, customizing, 246–247
AutoPreview option, 159
AutoRecover feature, customizing, 237
AutoShapes
    drawing, 125
    formatting, 128–129

## B

background command, 99
A Bit Better Corporation, 267
black and white
    printing, 198
    viewing slides, 152
black screen, 226
blue items in Task panes, 11

bold. *See* styles, text.
bold text. *See* styles, text.
Brainy Betty, 269
Broadcast feature, 204
browser support
    fonts, 213
    Web presentations, 205, 210, 213
bullet lists, 44–45, 53

## C

cAPS LOCK key option, 245
charts
    default type, changing, 77
    formatting, 77
    inserting, 76–77
    placeholders, 72
"Click to add text?" message, 37
clip art. *See also* drawings; graphics; pictures.
    inserting, 78–79
    inserting in slides, 122–123
    Microsoft online collection, 123
    online resources, 123, 270
    placeholders, 72
    searching for, 122–123
    sound clips, 123
Clipart.com, 269
Color dialog box, 99
Color Schemes task pane, 94
colors
    for all slides, 96
    displaying, 94
    editing, 98–99
    for single slides, 95
    text, 38–39. *See also* styles, text.
    Web presentations, 214–215
commands, images for, 249
Compare and Merge Presentation feature, 220–221
Compress Picture tool, 135
configuring
    AutoCorrect, 244–245
    files, 234–235
    presentations
        AutoCorrect settings, 244–245
        AutoFormat settings, 246–247
        automatic links to URLs, 247
        AutoRecover feature, 237
        default layout for new slides, 239
        editing settings, 240–241
        file properties, 234–235
        images for commands, 249
        menus, 248–249

# Index

flipping, 131
formatting, 128–129
geometric shapes, 126
grids, 138–139
grouping/ungrouping, 136
guides, 138–139
moving, 130, 140
nudging, 140
rearranging, 137
resizing, 130
rotating, 131
stacking in layers, 137
text boxes, 127
WordArt, 132–133
Duplicate Slide feature, 145, 148
duplicating slides, 145, 148

## E

editing
  color schemes, 98–99
  keyboard shortcuts for, 259
  outlines, 61
  settings, customizing, 240–241
  tables, 74–75
  text, 36–37
e-mailing presentations for review, 219
embossing text. *See* styles, text.
end PowerPoint. *See* exit PowerPoint.
execute PowerPoint. *See* start PowerPoint.
exit PowerPoint, 6–7

## F

fact checking. *See* research.
felt tip pen, 228–229
files
  customizing, 234–235
  Properties dialog box, 234–235
  size, and slide shows, 185
fill patterns, 129
finding. *See* searching for.
fixed-width fonts, 212–213
flipping drawings, 131
folder location
  finding, 21, 26–27
  saving to, 21
Font dialog box *versus* Formatting toolbar, 39
fonts. *See also* styles, text.
  browser compatibility, 213
  fixed-width, 212–213
  proportional, 212–213

slide designs, 85
text, 40–41
Web presentations, 212–213
formatting
  automatic correction. *See* AutoFormat; Smart Tags.
  AutoShapes, 128–129
  drawings, 128–129
  tables, 75
  text
    bullet lists, 44–45
    color, 38–41
    fonts, 40–41
    Formatting toolbar *versus* Font dialog box, 39
    raised/lowered, 39
    scientific notation, 39
    size, 40–41
    style, 38–41
    subscripts, 39
    superscripts, 39
Formatting toolbar *versus* Font dialog box, 39

## G

General tab, 235
geometric shapes, drawing, 126
graphic elements, slide designs, 85
graphics. *See also* clip art; drawings; pictures.
  editing, 134–135
  inserting from files, 124
  online resources, 268–269
  in outlines, 53
graphs (charts)
  default type, changing, 77
  formatting, 77
  inserting, 76–77
  placeholders, 72
grayscale
  printing, 198
  viewing slides, 152
grids, 138–139
grouping/ungrouping objects, 136
guides, 138–139

## H

Handout Master, 118. *See also* Notes Master; Slide Master.
handouts, 196–197
hardware graphics acceleration, 183
headings, outlines
  rearranging, 57
  *versus* slide content, 53

# Index

# Index

# Index

# Index

displaying, 186
displaying multiple, 25
drawing on the screen, 228–229
ending, 186
excluding slides, 181
felt tip pen, 228–229
file size, 185
finding, 21, 26–27
folder location
  finding, 21, 26–27
  saving to, 21
hardware graphics acceleration, 183
Help, 231
highlighting pen, 228–229
ink pointer, 228–229
interacting with, 186
keyboard shortcuts, 260
loops, 179
multiple monitors, 182–183
narrations, 184–185, 223
navigating, 186, 224
online. *See* Web presentations.
opening, 22
options, setting, 178–179
organizing. *See* outlines; Slide Sorter.
overview of topics. *See* summary slides.
packaging, 187
passwords, 253
performance, 181
pointer, 228–229
printing
  black and white, 198
  custom settings, 193
  framing slides, 195
  grayscale, 198
  handouts, 196–197
  hidden slides, 199
  landscape orientation, 192
  multiple slides per page. *See* handouts.
  Notes Pages, 200
  number of pages, previewing, 191
  orientation, 192–193
  Outline view, 200
  output off center, 193
  page setup, 192–193
  portrait orientation, 192
  Print Preview, 190–191
  selected slides, 194
  speaker notes, 200
rehearsals, 222

reviewing
  applying changes, 220–221
  Compare and Merge Presentation feature, 220–221
  consolidating changes, 221
  e-mailing, 219
  proofreading, 222
  sending for review, 218–219
  tracking changes, 218–219, 220–221, 236–237
  unapplying changes, 221
  what the reviewer sees, 219
running, 186
saving, 20–21
saving for the road, 223
saving periodically, 237
sharing, keyboard shortcuts, 262
show type, selecting, 178–179
site preview, 223
slide advancement methods, 168, 171, 225. *See also* transitions.
speaker notes, 182–183, 227
starting/ending, 224
structure
  content slides, 30
  summary slides, 30
  title and text slides, 30
  title slides, 30
timing, 222
white screen, 226
Slide Sorter view
  description, 9
  resize slides, 35
  show more slides, 35
slides. *See also* presentations; slide shows.
  adding, 32
  advancement methods, 168, 171. *See also* transitions.
  advancing. *See* transitions.
  content, 30
  copy and paste, 145
  default layout for new, 239
  deleting
    Normal view, 33–34
    Slide Sorter view, 146
  duplicating, 145, 148
  hiding, 149
  hiding formatting, 147
  moving, 144
  navigating, 35–36
  printing
    black and white, 198
    custom settings, 193
    framing, 195

# Index

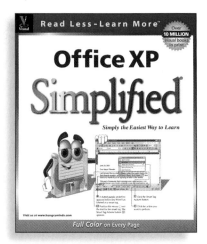

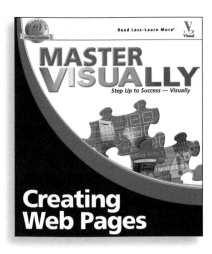

# ...all designed for visual learners—just like you!

## Top 100 Simplified® Tips & Tricks

Tips and techniques to take your skills beyond the basics. Full color.

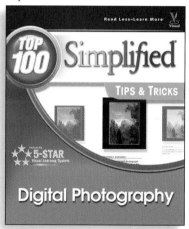

## Visual Blueprint™

Where to go for professional level programming instruction. Two-color.

**Read Less—Learn More®**

### For a complete listing of Visual books, go to wiley.com/go/visualtech

### Also available:

- Windows XP: Top 100 Simplified Tips & Tricks, 2nd Edition
- Photoshop Elements 3: Top 100 Simplified Tips & Tricks
- Mac OS X v.10.3 Panther: Top 100 Simplified Tips & Tricks
- eBay: Top 100 Simplified Tips & Tricks
- HTML: Top 100 Simplified Tips & Tricks
- Office 2003: Top 100 Simplified Tips & Tricks
- Excel 2003: Top 100 Simplified Tips & Tricks
- Photoshop CS: Top 100 Simplified Tips & Tricks
- Internet: Top 100 Simplified Tips & Tricks

### Also available:

- HTML: Your visual blueprint for designing effective Web pages
- Excel Programming: Your visual blueprint for creating interactive spreadsheets
- Unix for Mac: Your visual blueprint to maximizing the foundation of Mac OS X
- MySQL: Your visual blueprint for creating open-source databases
- Active Server Pages 3.0: Your visual blueprint for developing interactive Web sites

- Visual Basic .NET: Your visual blueprint for building versatile programs on the .NET Framework
- Adobe Scripting: Your visual blueprint for scripting in Photoshop and Illustrator
- JavaServer Pages: Your visual blueprint for designing dynamic content with JSP
- Access 2003: Your visual blueprint for creating and maintaining real-world databases

# Want instruction in other topics?

## Check out these

### All designed for visual learners—just like you!

Read Less—Learn More®

Teach Yourself VISUALLY
Yoga
The Fast and Easy Way to Learn
0-7645-2580-8

Read Less-Learn More®
Teach Yourself VISUALLY
The Fast and Easy Way to Learn
Windows XP
2nd Edition
Covers Windows XP Service Pack 2!
Over 120 Pages in FULL COLOR
0-7645-7927-4

Read Less-Learn More®
Teach Yourself VISUALLY
The Fast and Easy Way to Learn
Mac OS X v.10.3 Panther
Over 300 Pages in FULL COLOR
0-7645-4393-8

**For a complete listing of *Teach Yourself VISUALLY*™ titles and other Visual books, go to wiley.com/go/visualtech**